MACHINE TRANSLATION THROUGH PIVOT LANGUAGES

CASE OF ARABIC-HINDI LANGUAGE PAIR

SYED AFROZ AHMED | NISHEETH JOSHI

Contents

About The Authors

Syed Afroz Ahmad is an Adjunct Faculty at University of Fujairah, UAE. He has over 20 years of teaching experience. His research area is Data Analytics, Machine Translaion, Natural Languaeg Processing and Internet of Things and have published several papers in this area. Dr Ahmad has also published a book on MS Excel.

Dr. Nisheeth Joshi is an Associate Professor at Banasthali Vidyapith, India. He has done his Ph.D. in the area of Natural Language Processing. Being involved in teaching and research for over 15 years, he has developed the art of explaining even the most complicated topics in a straight forward and lucid manner. He also has vast experience in handling large scale research projects. This has helped him in developing practical insights into complex AI systems.

He is the recipient of the prestigious ISTE-U.P. Government National Award for Outstanding Work Done in Specified Areas of Engineering and Technology. He has authored several papers in international journals and conferences of repute. The topics on which he has published include Machine Translation Evaluation, POS Tagging, Morphology, Named Entity Recognition, Text Simplification etc. He has authored three books and two MOOCs. Two of his books have been translated into Chinese and one has been translated into Korean.

Dr. Joshi has also been an active reviewer who regularly reviews papers from Computer Speech and Language (Elsevier), International Journal for Intelligent Systems (Wiley), IEEE Access, IEEE Transactions on Cognitive and Developmental Systems, ACM Transactions on Asian and Low Resource Language Information Processing and Journal of Theoretical and Experimental Artificial Intelligence (Taylor and Francis). He is also a member of technical programme committees of International Conferences being organized in India and abroad. Some of these conferences are in their $15^{th}/16^{th}$ editions.

Dr. Joshi has also been a mentor and consultant to various start-ups working in the area of Cognitive Computing, Natural Language Processing, Speech Processing, Multimodal Information Retrieval and Machine Translation. He was also a consultant to C-DAC Pune where he developed the evaluation methodology for Mantra Machine Translation System. This Machine Translation System is being used by Rajya Sabha, the Upper House of Parliament of India and Department of Official Languages, Government of India. He has two technology transfers and four copyrights to his credit.

Preface

Machine Translation (MT) is a type of language translation in which a computer program is used to translate text or speech from one language to another. The translation is done automatically by an algorithm, instead of a human translator. This can be done from text-to-text or speech-to-text. MT is becoming increasingly popular as it is cost-effective, fast and accurate.

Who this book is for

This book is for researchers and enthusiasts who wish to work in the area of machine translation and wsih to unerstand how pivot based machine translation works.

To get the most out of this book

The prerequisites of this book are that you should have an unerstanding of Natural Language Processing (NLP) and Machine Translation (MT). You should have taken a course in either of them.

Prologue

Machine Translation has been one of the prominent areas of research in Artificial Intelligence (AI) and Natural Language Processing (NLP). Although this area has seen a lot of research and we have achieved some major breakthroughs, but still a fully automatic high-quality machine translation remains a distant possibility. One of the major reasons is the lack of resources in the languages for which the translation is to done. One major bottleneck is lack of availability of parallel corpus. In this research, we have tried to address this issue. When we don't have parallel corpus available corpus available for a particular language pair then how can we implement a machine translation system for it.

We have addressed this issue by using pivot language for performing machine translation. For our study, automatic translation between Arabic and Hindi. As such, there was no parallel corpus available for this language pair, but there was parallel corpus available for Arabic-English language pair and also for English-Hindi. Thus, English was used a pivot (intermediate) language for implementing machine translation system between Arabic-Hindi. Here, we implemented two MT engines. One for Arabic-English and the other for English-Hindi. Similarly, this was also done for Urdu as parallel corpus was available for Arabic-Urdu and Urdu-Hindi language pairs. Our main goal behind this was that Urdu is a more related to Arabic and Hindi as compared to English. Next, we used a combination of intermediate (pivot) languages for performing Arabic-Hindi machine translation. For this we used two MT systems. The first system used English as first and Urdu as second pivot language and the second system used Urdu as first and English as second pivot language.

For these four MT systems, we used five MT methodologies and implemented 5 MT systems for each pivot pair languages. In all we developed 10 MT engines for one pivot pair and overall, we developed 50 MT engines for all pivot pairs implemented for all MT methodologies. We also evaluated the results of our experiments using human and automatic evaluation metrics. For human evaluation we have HEval human evaluation metric which evaluated the MT output for semantic adequacy and we employed BLEU and Meteor as automatic evaluation metrics. These two are one of the most popular automatic evaluation metrics. They were used as we also wish to identify as which automatic evaluation metric works well with which pivot pair. As while developing MT system, waiting for human evaluation takes a lot of time. Thus, an MT system manager has to rely on automatic evaluation metric for rapid development of MT system. In our study we have identified this automatic metric which can produce better results for Arabic-Hindi language pair. We found that BLEU in almost all the accounts work better than Meteor. To our surprise, English was a better pivot language than Urdu or the combination of the two. This contradicted our initial assumption that related language can a better choice as a pivot language. One possible reason for this could be the lack of availability of large corpus for training MT systems.

CHAPTER ONE

Introduction

Since the dawn of time, language has been one of the important activities in the evolution of mankind. As the communities grew and became aware of other communities, trading between them started. The traders, who went to far-flung areas, were required to sell their products in a language that they did not know. Thus, emerged the importance of translation. Since the mid-20th century, computing emerged as a forerunner in technology development. With an increase in processing, the computer systems were able to do the automatic translation. This was known as machine translation (MT) or Machine Aided Translation (MAT).

Over the years MT has improved many folds, but it is still yet to achieve fully automatic high-quality machine translation status. A lot of approaches have been introduced to implement MT systems. All these approaches have their pros and cons. This is the reason why having a fully autonomous MT system is a distant dream.

In this thesis, we have tried to address the issues of current MT systems by using a Pivot language-based approach for MT. In this approach, an intermediate natural language is used between the source and the target language. For our study, we have used the Arabic-Hindi language pair. The reason for selecting this pair is due to its lack of availability of parallel corpus. Thus, in order or implement an MT system for this language pair, we need to implement it using an intermediate language. For our study, we have used English and Urdu as the intermediate (pivot) languages.

1.1 History of Machine Translation

The first documented instance of automatic translation or machine translation was in the early 1950s when IBM attempted to translate Russian sentences into English. For this, they used a bi-lingual Russian-English dictionary. This experiment is also popularly known as the Georgetown experiment. In this, IBM used six rules for performing the translation.

This attracted public attention to this field of study. In particular, this got hold of the US government's attention which wanted to quickly perform translations of Russian text into English. Due to this experiment, a lot of research funding was put in by the Department of Defense, USA. Unfortunately, this experiment and several initial experiments like these performed very well in lab settings but failed to perform in real-life scenarios. After more than ten years of funding, when good results were not produced then the US government appointed a committee to review the funding in this area. The committee was popularly known as the Automatic Language Processing Advisory Committee (ALPAC). It was formed in 1964 and it gave its report in 1966. In that report, the committee suggested that with the current state of the art in computing facilities, it was not possible to develop a fully automatic high-quality machine translation (FAHQT) system. Thus, they suggested that instead of putting money into MT, it would be advisable to provide funding to core natural language processing (NLP) tasks which would strengthen the foundation areas of MT. This report also had an impact on the work being done in the United Kingdom (UK) and then the erstwhile USSR.

With the report of the ALPAC committee, the work on MT development almost came to a standstill in the US, UK, and USSR. Although, people in France, Canada, and Germany kept working in this area. In 1969-70, an MT company in the US (SYSTRAN Inc.) was established. They kept improving the IBM Georgetown experiment. Due to this, they pocketed a major US Air Force contract on MT in the early 1970s. In 1977, Université de Montréal developed an MT system for Canadian Metrological Department which translated weather forecasts from English to French. These systems heavily relied on rule-based MT (RBMT). In the late 1970s, mainframe computers were used for building MT systems.

In the 1980s, with the advancement of personal computers, several rule-based MT systems were developed. In the early 1980s, new technology on MT was developed by the Japanese. Later on, this was termed as Example-Based MT (EBMT). With the advancement of this technique, several EBMT systems were developed.

With the dawn of the current century, EBMT systems were transformed into Statistical MT systems. In the late 2000s, several SMT systems developed the world over. Around 2012, Neural MT (NMT) was introduced by Google Inc. Since then there have been many advancements in this area. Even companies like SYSTRAN shifted their focus from the RBMT to the

NMT approach. Figure 1.1 summarizes this entire history.

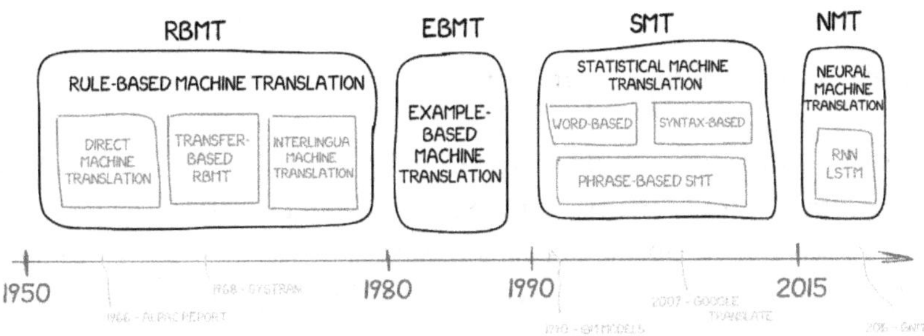

Figure 1.1: History of Machine Translation

A summary of SMT

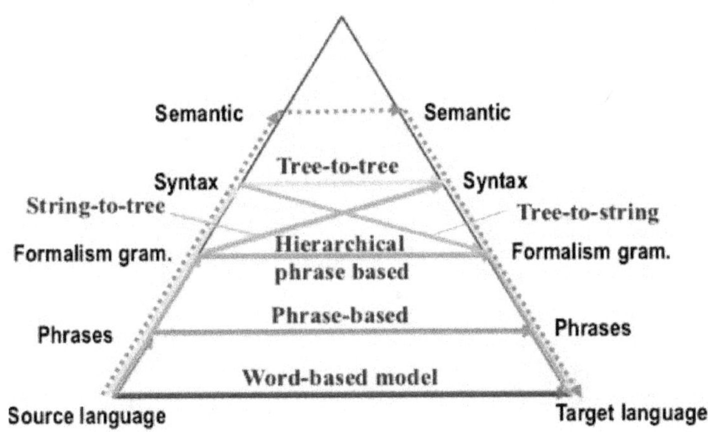

Figure 1.2: Approaches to Machine Translation

1.2 Approaches to Machine Translation

There are several approaches through which we can develop an MT system. Figure 1.2 shows these approaches. In this section, we shall provide a brief explanation of these approaches.

Word-Based Machine Translation

In this approach, a simple word-to-word mapping was done to produce machine translation. In this approach, a bi-lingual dictionary is used to perform the translation. Sometimes these translation systems have a word reordering procedure in place, which preserves the meaning incorporated in the original sentence. For Example, suppose we have an English sentence as "This is a beautiful morning." The word-to-word translation of this is shown in Table 1.1

Source Word (English)	Target Word (Hindi)
This	यह
Is	है
A	एक
beautiful	खूबसूरत
morning	दिन
.	।

Table 1.1: Word-to-Word Translation Example

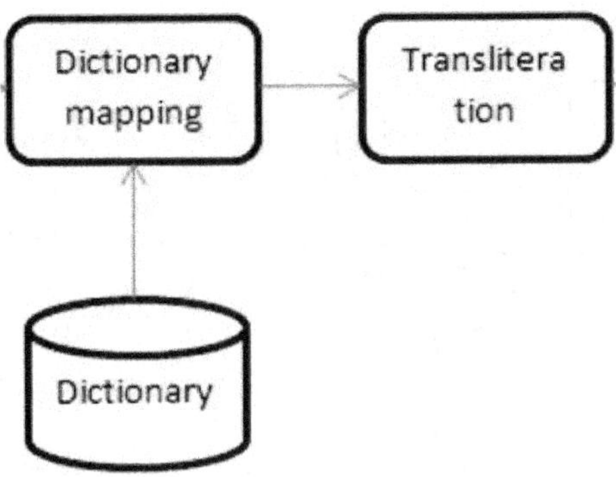

Figure 1.3: Word-to-Word (Dictionary) Based Machine Translation

The translation of this sentence can be produced as it is with little or no reordering. These were the very first MT systems. Figure 1.3 shows the working of this approach.

Example-Based Machine Translation

In this approach, we are provided with a database/knowledge base of example translations. When we get a new sentence for translation, we first search for possible partial translation matches. Once the matches are found, we apply an alignment and recombination algorithm which can capture the syntax of the target language. Once this is done, the result as produced as a translation. Figure 1.4 shows this approach.

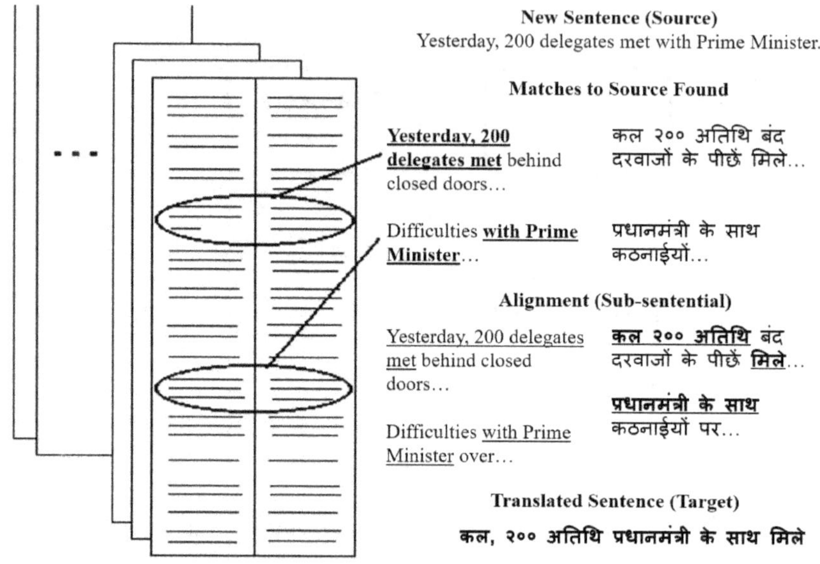

Figure 1.4: Working of Example-Based Machine Translation

- **Statistical Machine Translation**

In this approach, the example translations of the previous approach are assigned probabilities and the translation is done using the noisy channel method used in automatic speech recognition (ASR). This is based on equation 1.

$$P(e|f) = Argmax((P(f|e) \; X \; P(e))$$
(1.1)

Here, e is the target language in which we wish to produce the translation

f is the source language which is given as an input

Argmax is the decoding algorithm

$P(f|e)$ is the translation model

$P(e)$ is the language model

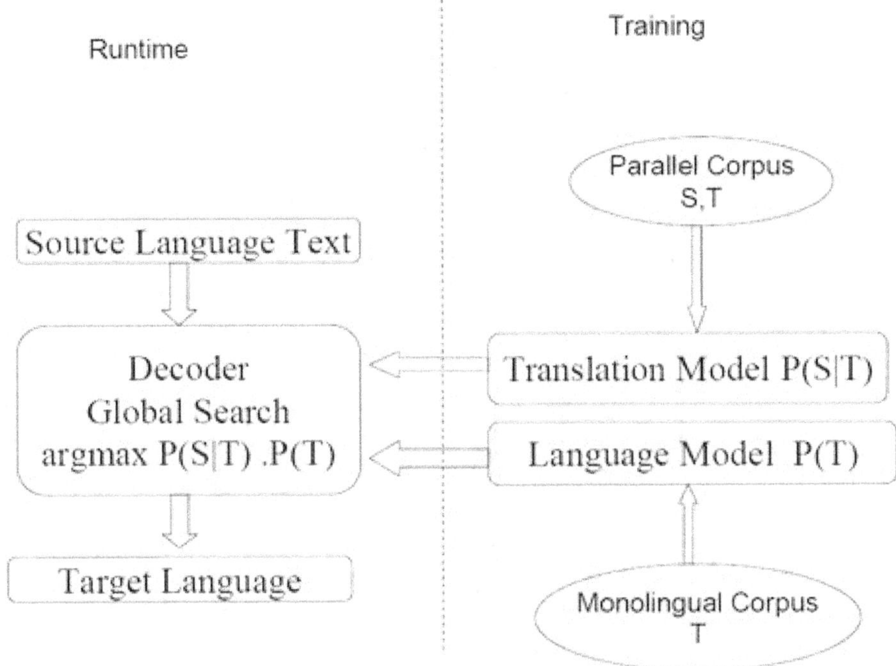

Figure 1.5: Working of Phrase-Based Machine Translation

In this translation methodology, our objective is to produce the best translation for a given source sentence. For this, we have a model available to us which has a pair of source and target language (translation model) and also has chunks of the target language (language model). Argmax finds the best translation pair produced by the combination of the translation model and language models. This model is also known as phrase-based machine translation (PBMT) Figure 1.5 shows the working of this translation system.

Hierarchical Machine Translation

This is an extension of PBMT where an intermediate grammar is also constructed for performing the translation. This is not the conventional context-free grammar (CFG) or dependency grammar (DG). Rather this form of grammar is termed hero grammar. This is a form of universal grammar. An example of this type of grammar is shown in figure 1.6

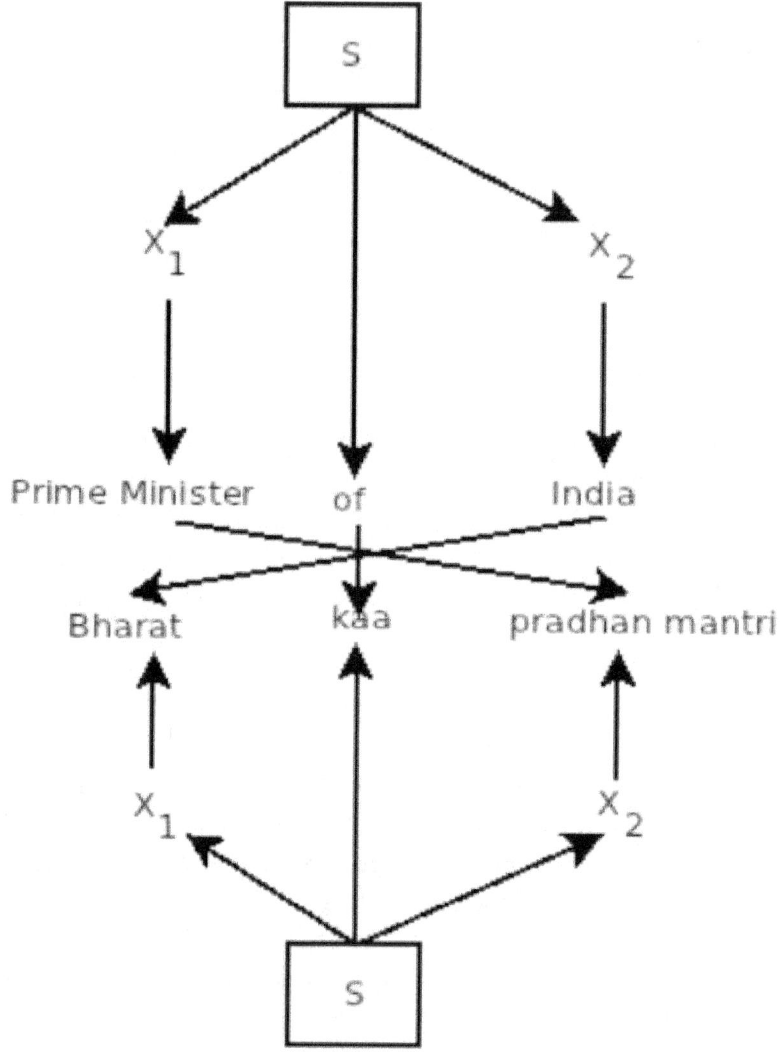

Figure 1.6: Example of Herio Grammar

Here, X1 and X2 are phrases that are aligned in the training corpus. Unlike PBMT, here this grammar rule is assigned probabilities. During execution, the target sentence is generated through this grammar.

Factored Machine Translation

This is another extension of PBMT where linguistic information is used to perform the translation. The working of this system is shown in figure 1.7. Here, along with phrases, morphological and part-of-speech (POS) information is also used in training the system. The same information is during execution while translating a sentence.

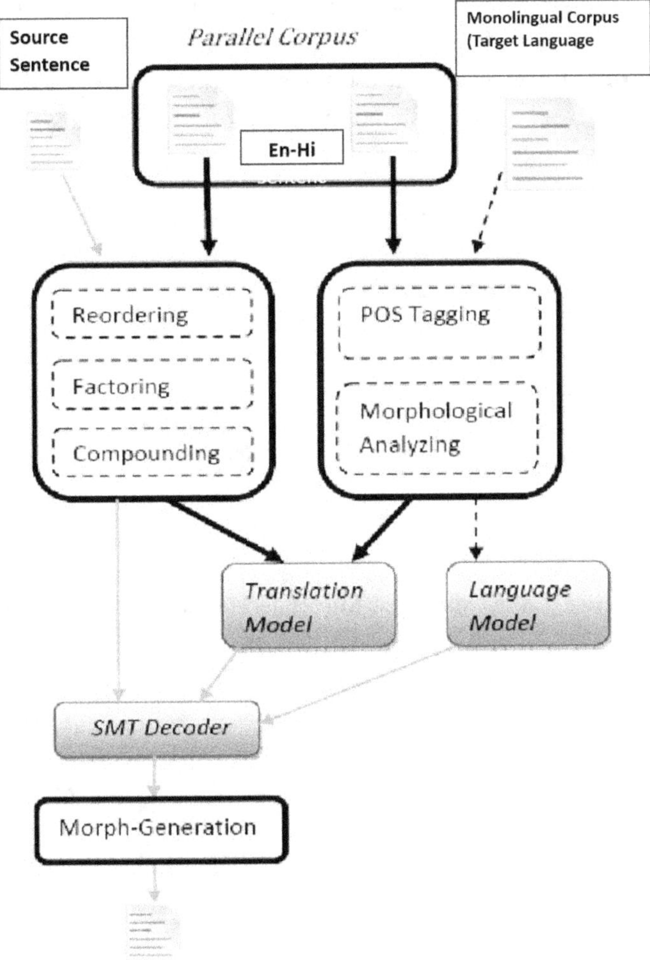

Figure 1.7: Example of Factored Machine Translation

Transfer-Based (Rule-Based) Machine Translation

In a transfer-based or rule-based MT. We use NLP tools for doing the translation. Essentially the entire translation system is divided into three phases. They are:

1. **Analysis Phase:** Here the source sentence is analyzed and syntactic processing is done.
2. **Transfer Phase:** Here the source syntax is transferred into the target structure.
3. **Generation Phase:** Here the target sentence is constructed from the target structure that is produced from the previous phase.

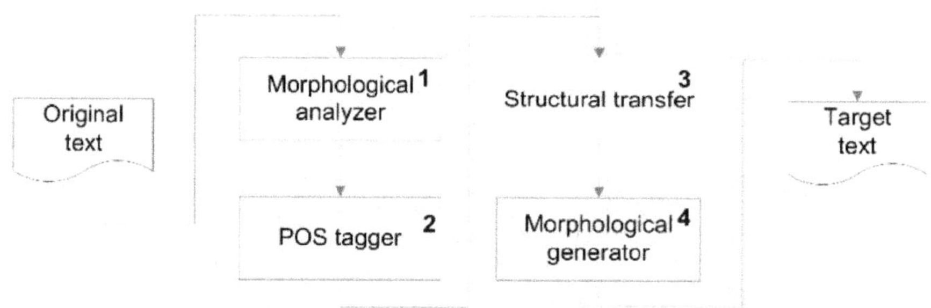

Figure 1.8: Example of Rule-Based Machine Translation

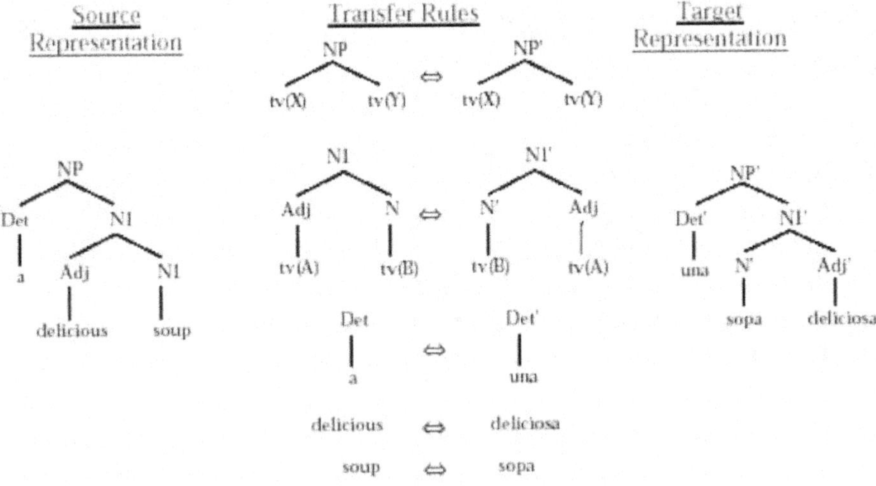

Figure 1.9: Example of Syntax Transfer in RBMT

Figure 1.8 shows the working of this system. Figure 1.9 shows how the source sentence's structure is transformed into the target structure.

Interlingua-Based Machine Translation

In the previous approaches, the basic problem was that if we have ten languages and we wish to develop MT systems in all these languages, then we need 10X9 = 90 MT systems. Suppose we increase the number of languages to 1000, then we need 1000X999 MT systems. Developing this huge inventory of MT systems is not an easy task. For quite some time a need is being felt to develop an approach to the MT system which can require this developmental bottleneck. In the late 1970s, an approach termed interlingua was proposed which can translate a sentence into an intermediate language and then can be translated into the target language, but to date, we do not have any language which is eligible to be this intermediate language.

1.3 Chapter Outline

This book has seven chapters. The first chapter is an introduction to the problem. This chapter also describes the approaches used in machine translation. Chapter two reviews the work is done in the area of pivot-based machine translation. Chapter three discusses the methods and materials required in our experiments. It describes the corpus used in developing and testing MT systems, linguistic resources used in MT systems. Various toolkits used in MT systems. The MT evaluation metrics used in our experiments. Chapter four discusses the development process and evaluation results of Arabic-Hindi MT using English as a pivot. Chapter five discusses the development process and evaluation results of Arabic-Hindi MT using Urdu as a pivot. Chapter six discusses the development process and evaluation of Arabic-Hindi MT using English and Urdu as pivot and Urdu and English as a pivot. Chapter seven concludes the entire work and provides future directions which can extend this research.

CHAPTER TWO

Review of Previous Work Done

Dayley (1983) presented a survey on voice and ergativity in Mayan languages. Their aim was to bring together data on voice and ergativity in the language family. **Muraki (1987)** has a patent on their work on a pivot-based system having a pragmatic table for detecting semantic structures. **Blelloch and Sabot (1990)** have described problems and methods for taking a detailed description of parallelism as operations on collections and then translating them into flat parallel form. **Okumura et al. (1991)** have proposed a strategy for French and Spanish systems generating sentences based on English systems. Using this approach, the authors have developed sentence generation systems for English, French, Korean and Spanish.

Darlington et al. (1994) have worked on the development of the Fortran-S system which is a practical structured parallel language completely compatible with established languages. **David (1994)** has proposed a novel method of decomposition that benefits from both the semantic properties of active constraints and the network's structural properties. **Lee (1996)** surveyed methods for learning the behavior of context-free languages, by considering negative results and 5 methods that take different inputs.

Borin (2000a) has reported on experiment series with pivot alignment by using additional languages to improve the bilingual alignment of words. **Borin (2000b)** has investigated a new information source which is- pivot language for increasing alignment recall. **Gey (2000)** has focussed on failure analysis and resource contribution for improvement in cross-language IR. **Hajic et al. (2000)** have argued that for closely related languages a better quality of translation can be achieved by easier methods using examples of Transfer -based MT system and word-for-word MT system.

Boite (2001) has proposed four keys to open a new gate of adequate quality for all languages in MT. These keys cover the technical, research, and organizational aspects for improving the quality of MT while handling more languages. **Bond et al. (2001)** have presented a technique for combining the Japanese-English and Malay-English dictionaries to make a third one using a pivot language. They have used semantic classes for ranking the translation equivalents. The approach prefers word pairs with compatible semantic classes.

Collins and Sanderson (2001) have reported on a new approach of parallel translation across multiple intermediate languages and result fusing. **Arka (2002)** considered the Austronesian language typology by observing their voice systems and voice markings. **Bright and Tsai (2002)** have developed a prototype where new users can directly interact in their own language with the goal of merging approaches of pivot MT, interactive MT, and multilingual text authoring. **Christy (2002)** has a patent on their work of translating and communicating a digital message using a third language as a pivot.

Lehtokangas and Airio (2002) have reported on transitive translation experiments where search topics were translated into document collection language using a bridge language. They have worked on Finnish and German languages with English as a pivot language. This approach had promising results. **Ballesteros & Sanderson (2003)** have provided strong empirical evidence for a combination of methods producing significant enhancement in effectiveness retrieval. **Euzenat and Stueken Schmidt (2003)** have presented the language family based on a collection of knowledge representation languages. The partial ordering of these languages is based on transformability from one language to another by conserving formal properties such as a logical consequences.

Kishida and Kando (2003) have reported on German to Italian cross-lingual information retrieval with an approach for resource-poor language. The approach uses the transitive translation of questions with English ads pivot language. **Homola and Kubon (2004)** have proposed a technique of translation between languages with syntactic similarity. It was based on the thought that in the case of related languages, the closeness would be exploited by easy methods. **Koehn and Monz (2005)** have described their goals, tasks, and resources for the ACL-2005 workshop hosted shared task on building SMT for 4 European language pairs.

Scheutz (2005) has explained the importance of pivot elements which are stored equally in MT. **Stroustrup (2005)** has presented a new approach by providing a library language that is semantically enhanced, expressive, maintainable, cost-efficient, and teaching. These languages were special purpose and were developed by super setting a language using a library and the further result is subsetted using a syntax and semantics understanding tool. **Wang et al. (2006)** have proposed an approach to enhance word alignment for resource-poor languages and used bilingual corpora of related languages as the pivot.

Babyeh et al. (2007) have compared two techniques for English translation from resource-poor languages. The first method is a direct transfer by using an already available MT system for the language pair. The second method uses a cognate language that is resource-rich for translation. A comparison shows the use of pivot language gives a better-quality translation.

Brauer and Demuth (2007) have proposed the use of a common pivot model for integrating the OCL standard library on the model level. They have adopted a declarative definition of already defined types and operations. This has improved the properties of reusability, maintainability, and flexibility to a great extent. This method has made OCL integration with domain-specific languages very easy. They have explained the uses and feasibility of this approach via examples. Their model lacks the power of expressing the model's dynamics semantics for OCL collections.

Utiyama and Isahara (2007) have compared phrase and sentence translation as two pivot strategies for phrase-based SMT. Phrase translation strategy involves the creation of phrase translation tables from the source to English language and other from English to the target language. Sentence translation involves translation from a source language to English to a target language. The highest-scoring sentences are selected from the target sentences. The Europarl corpus was used to evaluate the performance of these strategies in comparison with SMT systems which are trained directly. The phrase translation strategy proved to be better than sentence translation strategy. The performance of the phrase translation strategy was 0.92 in comparison to 0.97 if directly trained SMT systems.

Wu and Wang (2007) have provided a novel method for phrase-based SMT which uses pivot language. They propose that by using only source to pivot and pivot to target bilingual corpora, a translation model for source to target can be developed. This proves helpful because we can do translation from source to target even in the absence of a bilingual corpus. They evaluated their approach by examining the coverage of phrase tables in comparison to the test phrases. According to the BLEU metric, this method achieves absolute improvements of 0.05 and 0.04 on the in-domain and out-domain testing set. The results indicate that more pivot languages can give better translation quality.

Bertoldi et al. (2008) have adopted two approaches for phrase-based pivot SMT. Approach 1 uses the pivot language at translation time while Approach 2 uses the pivot language at the training time. They have used Moses and a statistical log-linear model with 8 features. They optimized the weights of their model by using a minimum error training process.

Tsunakawa et al. (2008a) have proposed a novel technique for constructing a bilingual lexicon using pivot language in phrase-based SMT. They used parallel corpora for two languages extracted the phrase tables and merged them into one final phrase table. Lastly, they constructed a phrase-based SMT for translating terms from the source-pivot lexicon into the target language and extracting a new source to the target lexicon. This experiment improved the utilization ratio of the corpora greatly.

Tsunakawa et al. (2008b) gave a technique for enhancing size of the bilingual lexicon obtained from two lexicons using pivot language. There are two main challenges to this approach: ambiguity and mismatch of terms. They have targeted the problem of term mismatch by improving ratio of utilization of bilingual lexicons. They computed probability of lexical translations of word pairs by using a statistical word-alignment model and term decomposition/composition techniques. They have also compared three approaches viz. exact merging, word-based merging, and alignment-based merging to generate the bilingual lexicon. Then they combined lexical translation probabilities and an easy language model for calculating translation pair probabilities. The results show that the proposed method enhances the utilization ratio of available bilingual lexicons.

Habash and Hu (2009) have presented a comparative study of Arabic-Chinese MT with English as a pivot language. The two compared approaches are sentence pivoting and phrase-table pivoting. The phrase table pivoting gives better results on the BLEU evaluation metric. They have considered orthographic, morphological, and syntactic linguistic issues divergent in English, Arabic, and Chinese. The results show that the use of Pivot language English outperforms direct translation.

Koehn et al. (2009) have constructed 462 MT systems for all language pairs of multilingual parallel JRC-Acquis corpus. They trained-tuned-tested these systems using the dataset developed during this experiment. They used the Moses toolkit with a maximum sentence length of 80 words, a bidirectional re-ordering model, and a 5-gram language model. They did a regression study to find out factors affecting the performance. They are morphological complexity, reordering, language relatedness, and size of the corpus.

Max (2009) has adopted a context-based approach. He has taken parallel multilingual corpora that detect small paraphrases by detecting appropriate pivot phrases in secondary languages and re-translating them in original languages and re-translating them in the original language. He has elaborated on using context to find pivot phrases and finding the most appropriate paraphrases. Paraphrasing can vary from a word to sub-sentential fragments. The distinctive feature of this approach is that it targets text fragments that can be larger than phrases that are traditionally targeted by statistical techniques.

Nakov and Ng (2009) proposed a novel approach independent of languages and aimed at improving SMT for resource-poor language. They tried improving translation by using the similarity of resource-poor languages to resource-rich languages by using a limited number of parallel sentences between both languages. Their BLEU score shows good gain in comparison to other approaches.

Ng et al. (2009) focussed on finding languages that are related closely. They have considered indigenous languages. The relationship between the languages is established via matching with the pivot language. For this orthographic approach is used where spelling matching is used.

Paul et al. (2009) have investigated the aptness of languages other than English as a pivot language. They considered 110 languages and their experiment showed that 61 out of 110 languages improved the quality of translation when a non-English language was used as a pivot. The Experiments show that an optimal pivot language is selected on the basis of source-pivot and pivot-source relationship is very important. Pivot selection criteria depend on the pivot-target relationship.

Tanaka et al. (2009) have observed problems like inconsistency, asymmetry, and intransitivity of selected words among different translation services. For this issue, they have proposed context-based coordination to maintain the actual meaning of words during pivot translations. In their first step, they generated multilingual equivalent terms based on dictionaries and use them for semantic preciseness. In the next step, a multi-agent architecture was shown as a method of implementation. In the system, a coordinating agent collects and executes contextual significance from the translation agent. The system was capable of identifying 58% of nouns and hence improved translation up to 40% at the sentence level.

Tsunakawa et al. (2009) have proposed an integrated framework for constructing a bilingual lexicon between Chinese and Japanese languages. These languages don't take English as their pivot languages so few large-scale resources have been developed between the two languages. They have used a bilingual lexicon via English in place of the pivot language, which has improved performance over the corpus-based approach.

Al-Hunaity et al. (2010) have also inspected a couple of pivot strategies for SMT between Danish and Arabic. These strategies are phrase translation and sentence translation. They have used English as their pivot language. They have developed two SMT systems, one for Danish-English and the other for English-Arabic. For the phrase translation strategy, they have constructed a Danish-Arabic phrase translation from the Danish-English phrase-table and an English-Arabic phrase table. According to their approach to translation, they first translated Danish sentences into a number of English sentences and then translated these English sentences and then translated these English sentences to Arabic. Then the highest-scoring sentence was selected. For phrase translation, they have directly constructed a Danish-Arabic phrase translation table from the phrase tables of Danish-English and English-Arabic. According to their experiment, the sentence-level translation outperforms the phrase-level translation.

Heidenrich et al. (2010) have argued that the discrepancy faced by OCL users needs to be addressed at a technical and methodological level. The paper gives a summary of technical basics to build integrated OCL tooling front and back end for random text modeling.

Leusch et al. (2010) have described a technique to exploit various pivot languages when using MT on language pairs with little bilingual resources or where no MT system is available. This technique can also be used where an MT system for a language pair is available but has low accuracy. They have shown that the direct MT approach can be replaced by a pivot translation system.

Liu et al. (2010) have presented TESLA and TESLA-M – automatic MT evaluation metrics with gold-standard performances. TESLA-M extends the benefits of METEOR and MaxSim and works on a more expressive linear programming framework. TESLA, on the other hand, exploits parallel texts to construct shallow semantic representations.

Otero and Campos (2010) have used existing resources to create new bilingual dictionaries. This approach is based on two tasks; first, a new set of bilingual correspondences is generated from two similar dictionaries that are available, and second, they have validated the correspondences generated by using an automatically extracted bilingual lexicon. They have reported a case study where a new and clean English-Galician dictionary was automatically generated with 12000 correct bilingual correspondences. This paper proposed an automatic lexicographic method whose main contribution is to use lexicon extracted from comparable corpora to validate the correspondences derived by transitivity. The main drawback of this approach is that it has to be language dependent because of the need for a syntactic parser to annotate the corpus. So, to make it work with many languages they have used a robust multilingual parser, DepPattern, developed by their team.

Vellecillo (2010) have discussed scenarios of some mechanisms of Domain-Specific Modelling Languages and proposed a general framework for combining DSMLs that subsumes them depending on the concept of unification of viewpoints.

Zhang et al. (2010) have presented two pivot strategies for SMT viz. system-based and model-based. The model-based strategy takes in independent source-pivot and pivot-target corpora and learns a direct source-target model of transliteration. Whereas the system-based strategy takes in a source-pivot model and a pivot-target model. Experiments show that a system-based pivot strategy is better than a model-based one because it effectively reduces the high resource requirements of training corpus for language pairs with lower densities.

Cettolo et al. (2011) have described their efforts toward developing an Arabic-Italian SMT system. They have worked in the news domain. Given the challenge of less available parallel data for the given pair of languages, they have compared the strategies of comparable corpora with that of using pivot languages.

Costa-Jussa et al. (2011) have opted to research the two most spoken languages Chinese and Spanish. They have explored different strategies for alternatives of SMT for the given language pair. The two famous alternatives are considered for pivoting: the cascade system and the pseudo-corpus method. They have used Arabic, French, and English as pivot languages. Their strategy was to use a combination of pivot methods and it successfully outperforms the direct translation strategy.

Dahlemeir et al. (2011) have described three flavors of TESLA: TESLA-M, TESLA-F, and the new TESLA-B. TESLA-M is the arithmetic average of F-measures between bags of n-grams. TESLA-B uses an average of two F-measure types-BTNG and BPNG. TESLA-F uses a general linear combination of three scores: BTNG F-measure, and BPNG. F-measure and normalize language model scores of the translation given by the system.

Paul and Sumita (2011) have provided a new understanding of what factors make good pivot languages and investigate the importance of these factors on the overall performance of translation by using pivot languages. Pivot-based experiments on SMT which translated between 22 Indo-European and Asian languages were utilized to fetch the impact of these factors. The results show that the factors identified by these researchers were capable of explaining 81% of the system performances and variations.

Paul et al. (2011) have proposed a novel technique of translating a dialect language into a foreign language by adopting different transliteration approaches which are based on the Bayesian co-segmentation model with the pivot SMT method. The proposed method has significantly improved the translation quality and has outperformed standard pivot translation approaches for most of the language pairs.

Saralegi et al. (2011) have observed in their work that on creating a source-to-target dictionary from source-pivot and pivot-target dictionaries we might get ambiguous words that are prone to wrong translations. They have analyzed two methods of pruning the wrong candidates, first, by analyzing the source dictionary structure and second, by computing distribution similarity from similar corpora. Both methods depend on easily available resources and are well-suited for low-resourced languages. Both methods successfully prune for a good number of frequent words. They face the issue of context representation for such words but perform well overall.

Steinberger et al. (2011) have presented a semi-automatic method of developing sentiment dictionaries in many languages. They approached this by first developing standard dictionaries of sentiment for two languages and then their translation into third languages. This paper has presented results after verifying this triangulation hypothesis. For verification, they evaluated the triangulated lists and compared them with a non-triangulated translated list of words.

Zhang et al. (2011) have investigated already existing systems and model-based strategies to find out the reason for worse performance by model-based strategy. They have proposed a joint alignment algorithm for optimizing transliteration alignments in a combination across the three languages- source-pivot and pivot-target. This improved the performance of a model-based strategy. They also proposed a new synthetic data-based model which is capable of generating source-target data with the involvement of pivot language. Results show that the collective-alignment optimization algorithm improves the accuracy of the model-based strategy and proved effective for pivot-based machine transliteration.

Di Ruscio et al. (2012) have focussed on architectural language interoperability. The paper aims on enhancing this using hierarchies of pivot languages taken up systematically by extension of a root pivot language. They have employed model-driven methods to support the development and management of hierarchies and to support the development and management of hierarchies and to implement interoperability through a transformation of the model.

Saralegi et al. (2012) have observed that bilingual dictionaries play important role in several areas of translation and NLP tasks. So, their development is crucial because they are only available for resource-rich languages. They proposed the development of automatic dictionaries by using pivot languages. This was done by merging the bilingual dictionaries of the source to pivot and pivot to target languages. They built Basque-Chinese automatic dictionary. Different methods were used to prune wrong translations. A manual evaluation of the dictionary was done and both Inverse Consultation and Distributional Similarity provides precise translations but poor recalls. Distribution similarity successfully prunes wrong translations for ambiguous words.

Nakov and Tiedemann (2012) have proposed techniques for the betterment of SMT between closely-related languages with few resources. They have used the n-gram bitexts approach for training character-level translation and tuned it using BLEU for word level. This was further augmented with character-based word-level transliteration and combined with a translation model for word level.

Nakov and Ng (2012) have proposed a new approach which is language-independent. This was aimed at improving MT for resource-poor languages by utilizing their similarity to major languages. They improved translation between resource-poor language and resource-rich language with a bi-text having limited parallel sentences for source-pivot translations while a larger bitext for target-pivot translations. The similarity between the two language pairs with respect to word order, spelling, and syntax and the vocabulary overlap help in improving word alignments for resource-poor language.

Tiedemann (2012) investigated the utilization of character-level models for translation. Their aim was to support translation involving closely related and low-resourced languages. Experimental results show that low-level models can prove successful with the use of small training data also. This approach was tested using legal data in a domain adaptation task and a movie dataset that has movie subtitles for three language pairs.

Acs et al. (2013) have explored various techniques for constructing bilingual dictionaries automatically. They observed that recent works using crowdsourced methods are stronger than techniques involving parallel and comparable corpora.

Hermann and Blunsom (2013) have combined the compositional semantics approach and shared word-level representations in their approach. They proposed a technique for learning distributed representations in a multi-lingual setup. Their model assigns similar embeddings to sentences aligned and dissimilar ones to sentences not aligned by learning.

Kim et al. (2013) have also proposed the construction of bilingual lexicons using a bridge language using the context-dependent approach. This is usually considered a standard approach. They have tried to represent context vectors in pivot language rather than target language which is the standard approach. This is a simplified approach and more accurate because it was parallel corpora. This experiment was performed on the Korean-Spanish language pair.

Kwon et al. (2013) presented a method for bilingual lexicon extraction in an automatic manner, using pivot language. They have utilized many IR and NLP techniques for the task. They have also worked on a word aligner which was freely available named, Anymalign. Using this software, they constructed context vectors. They did experiments on 2 language pairs i.e. Korean-Spanish and Korean-French both of which are bi-directional. Results explain that their high-frequency word approach performs better than other approaches.

Noren and Linell (2013) have collected six articles about a family of grammatical constructions from daily conversations as per their appearance in 5 different languages using English as a pivot.

Paul et al. (2013) have dug into the factors that make a pivot language effective and efficient. They measured the impact of these factors over state-of-the-art SMT techniques and found that these factors improved the translation quality of 54.8% of language pairs when a non-English pivot was used.

Ramirez et al. (2013) have presented the results of their research aimed at developing an automatic thesaurus for multiple languages which is based on Wikipedia and WordNet. Their aim was to increase resources for tasks like pivot-based MT and other NLP tasks involving resource-poor languages.

Salehi and Cook (2013) have presented a simple and effective technique of MWEs which is language-independent. They have compared the translations of an MWE with those of its components by using a range of different languages and measures of string similarity. They have explained the phenomena of two types of MWEs in English i.e. Nouns and Verbs. The results prove that their approach outperforms the state-of-the-art systems.

Wushouer et al. (2013) have proposed a novel method for creating MRDs for low-resourced languages. They have used a heuristic framework to induce a one-to-one mapping dictionary of a language pair that is closely related. This would use the dictionaries available for the languages involved.

Zhu et al. (2013) proposed a new approach that works on ML and enhances SMT based on pivot languages. For resource-poor languages, pivot-based translation has proved to be very effective. However, some useful source-target translations are not generated in some cases. In order to eliminate this problem, they have utilized Markov Random Walks to join candidate translation phrases among the source and target language.

El Kholy et al. (2013a) have proposed 2 features which are language-independent in nature, to improve phrase-pivot-based SMT, because even though pivoting is a robust process it gives few low-quality translations.

El Kholy et al. (2013b) have proposed a particular combination approach that is selective. This approach is selective. This approach includes pivot and direct SMT models to improve translation quality. They have worked on Persian Arabic SMT and their approach shows promising results along with a huge reduction in pivot translation model size.

Acs (2014) has explained a technique for enhancing existing dictionaries in a few languages by finding previously not-existing links among translations. This method of triangulation is presented by the authors and several variations are compared together. Precision is assessed manually. He has trained the Maximum Entropy classifier to check correct translations in noisy data.

Aker et al. (2014) have observed that the bilingual dictionaries developed by using the GIZA++ tool have a lot of noise due to which the output of techniques relying on dictionaries is negatively affected. So, they present three methods for denoising automatically developed bilingual dictionaries. These 3 approaches are LLR, pivot, and transliteration. These were applied to GIZAA++ dictionaries to remove noise. Their experiment shows that transliteration shows the best performance.

Dholakia and Sarkar (2014) have studied the triangulation for four languages that are low-resourced. They have improved the quality of translation by adding pivot language and comparing previous triangulation design options. They have utilized insights from domain adaptation to refine a weighted mixture of direct phrase pairs and pivot-based phrase pairs to improve the quality of translation.

El Kholy and Habbash (2014) observed that a significant step in SMT is combining bidirectional alignments into one alignment model called symmetrization. They have presented the relaxation of symmetrization heuristic to improve the phrase-pivot SMT quality. They have shown positive results on Hebrew-Arabic SMT with pivot as the English language.

Moulinier (2014) has performed monolingual and bilingual experiments for pivot language retrieval.

Seo et al. (2014) have proposed a new technique for building such lexicons for resource-poor language pairs. They have used two parallel corpora and a pivot language between them to construct these dictionaries. The experiment's accuracy is better than other methods of this kind.

Wushouer et al. (2014) have proposed a constraint optimization model to generate new dictionaries of languages that are closely related. They used various input dictionaries and their formalization. Evaluation results show that this technique outperforms the baseline along with performance improvement and scalability.

Zhu et al. (2014) have presented a new technique to calculate translation probability by pivoting the co-occurrence count of S-P and P-T phrase pairs. Experimental results outperform the baseline.

Dabre et al. (2015) have presented their work on leveraging multilingual parallel corpora of small sizes for SMT between Japanese-Hindi. They have used multiple pivot languages. In this setting, they kept the source and target as same. They have shown that using different pivots for phrase extraction from source and target parts results in great improvements. They adopted the method of Multiple Decoding Path (MDP) which results to be the best as compared to other methods.

Linard et al. (2015) have focussed on the extent to which the pivot language could be useful t bypass the original alignment. They defined two alignment approaches that involve bridge languages and then evaluated four languages and two pivot languages in particular. This enhanced the quality of extracted lexicon in a few cases.

Miura et al. (2015) have proposed a new methodology where in the triangulation stage pivot phrase are remembered. In this approach pivot language model is used as an additional information source at the time of translation.

More et al. (2015) have attempted to cater to two famous issues of SMT: the morphological difference between two languages and the inadequacy of parallel corpora. They have used word segmentation and pivots on languages that are morphologically complex. They have worked on Malayalam-Hindi SMT and have used triangulation as a pivoting strategy in addition to pre-processing based on morphology. Their approach performed 58% better than the baseline.

Zhang et al. (2015) have observed that in community-based QA, question retrieval is a challenge. The difficulty is the word mismatch between queries and candidate queries. Since existing methods have not considered the conceptual aspect, the authors have explored the pivot language translation approach to extract conceptual information. They have proposed a unified query retrieval model which includes concepts and paraphrases for the query. This approach outperforms the state-of-the-art model.

Kholy and Habash (2016) have examined the concept of synchronous morphology constraint feature. This helps in improving the quality of phrase pivot SMT. They compared tailor-made constraints with the ones that are fetched from parallel data in limited quantities between source-target languages. The morphological constraints learned to depend upon projected alignments amongst source and target phrases in the pivot phrase table. They worked on Hebrew-Arabic SMT with English as the pivot language.

Wushouer et al. (2016) have observed that the usual involvement of a third language has never been explained to utilize the complete structure of input bilingual dictionaries and this is an important failure because it impacts the result. They have designed a tool that implements their methods and outperforms the baseline.

Zhang et al. (2016) have explored an approach that identifies the key concepts for refining questions and translates using a pivot language. This helps in exploring key concept paraphrasing. They proposed a new model of question retrieval which flawlessly integrates concepts with their paraphrases.

Cheng et al. (2017) have proposed a pivot-based neural MT for resource-poor languages in which the source pivot and pivot target languages will be jointly trained in the system. This approach gives significant improvements over independently trained approaches across various languages.

Nakayama and Nishida (2017) have proposed constructing an NMT without supervised resources. They have used a multimodal representation of texts and images. They used multimedia as a pivot by projecting all modalities into a common space so that semantic concepts come closer to each other. This proved to be the key aspect of increasing closeness between different modalities. They also added a decoder to the model to enable the network to draw outputs from any input modality.

Nasution et al. (2017) have introduced a hybrid approach for pivot-based MT by combining SMT and RBMT because of the ethnic characteristics of Indonesian languages. They used Indonesian as their pivot language. This approach was evaluated for quality of translation, adequacy, and fluency to determine the usability of the system and the approach successfully improved the performance of other systems.

Nguyen et al. (2017) have proposed the very first online contributive lexical database system – PIVAX which allows to creation, maintain and manage lexical resources using a lexical pivot. PIVAX requires only the most basic language-specific lexical information to be stored in it, for the users to protect their proprietary information. Its design has reduced the unsolvable issue of creating a universal lexical database that is capable of supporting the lexical data or arbitrary set of MT systems. PIVAX is written over a generic jibiki platform and has evolved from a hypertextual PRAX multilingual database.

Creutz (2018) release Opusparcus-a new corpus for paraphrasing for six European languages. This corpus has sentence pairs in the same language with the almost same meaning. It has large training sets having millions of sentence pairs and was automatically compiled with the help of probabilistic ranking functions.

Liu et al. (2018) have reviewed the performances of pivot-based MT on a standard corpus using Chinese and English as pivot languages. They found that even though languages were very different, direct MT outperformed pivot-based MT. Results show that it would be beneficial to choose a pivot language closer to the source and target language. They also found that pivoting errors get propagated in target languages.

Mace et al. (2018) have presented a monitoring framework- Pivot Tracing, for distributed systems that address limitations of diagnosis tools by combining dynamic instrumentation with happen-before join. They have shown that Pivot Tracing is dynamic and can be extended and enables cross-tier analysis with the least overheads.

McCoy & Frank (2018) have used the Edit distance algorithm to process low-resourced languages. They presented 3 methods for evaluating the edit distance algorithm based on linguistic information. They also proposed a novel technique to assess the string similarity metrics depending on how much it enhances the performance.

Nasution et al. (2018) observed that while creating bilingual dictionaries linking several languages, its manual creation by a native speaker needs to be taken care of in case MRDs are not available. They have taken care of all such factors and proposed a new approach that collaborates constraint-based and plan-optimizer approaches for creating ten bilingual dictionaries by combinations of 5 languages. They also defined a heuristic plan that uses manual work only by native speakers. This plan outperformed the baseline with a 63.3% reduction in cost.

Prabhumoye et al. (2018) took the challenge of style transfer where an attribute of a sentence is transferred while keeping the meaning intact and keeping a balance between both. They proposed two extensions of standard-style transfer models with the goal of improving transfer accuracy.

Wushouer et al. (2018) observed that the regular approach of bilingual lexicon extraction was not capable of calculating semantic distance amongst bilingual word pairs. They discussed a constraint approach to pivot-based lexicon induction where target language pairs are closely related. They have created constraints from language similarity.

Bakshaei et al. (2019) have proposed a generative LDA-based model to fetch parallel fragments from similar documents without using any parallel corpus. Results show improvement if words are extracted by using the proposed method. The accuracy of the proposed method is 59.7%.

Nasution et al. (2019) have given an approach of developing language similarity groups and then generating clusters hierarchically with total linking and extracting high similarity to stable clusters. They introduced extended means clustering along with semi-supervised learning. According to their hypothesis, the higher the number of trials, the higher the chances of finding two hierarchically stable clusters.

Singhoff et al. (2019) have discussed various favourable and unfavourable points of ADLS (Architecture Description Language) from the point of view of scheduling analysis of RTCs that are dedicated for analysis.

CHAPTER THREE

Experimental Setup

In this chapter, we have discussed the resources and tools that were required to complete our research. We shall discuss the corpus used in this study, NLP resources that were used, and MT toolkits.

1. The equation of SMT and its Explanation
2. Equation of FMT and its Explanation
3. The equation of HPBMT and its Explanation
4. The equation for EBMT and its Explanation

3.1 Corpus Used

To perform machine translation for the Arabic-Hindi language pair via pivot languages, our first task was to select the corpus for the X language, in which Arabic text will be converted. Next, our task was to select the corpus, where the text in language X was converted into Hindi. We choose two languages for our intermediate language X. These were English and Urdu. Thus, we have four MT frameworks via these pivot languages.

For Arabic-English, we used the UN corpus (Ziemski, 2016) which had the official documents and parliamentary proceedings of the UN available in the public domain. For our purpose, we downloaded only the Arabic-English language pair. This has 1,85,39,207 parallelly aligned sentences, out of which, we used 18,53,921 sentences as our training corpus and 9,26,960 sentences as our tuning corpus.

For Arabic-Urdu, we used QCRI corpus (Abdelali, 2014) which had parallelly aligned sentences from the online educational material. These were taken from Udacity[1], Coursera[2], Khan Academy[3] and TED Talks[4]. This has a total of 1,85,000 sentences, out of which we used 1,48,000 sentences as training corpus and 37,000 sentences as tuning corpus.

For English-Hindi, Urdu-Hindi, and English-Urdu language pairs, we used the EILMT corpus (Lata et al., 2012) which had tourism-related documents developed under the project, "Development of English to Indian Languages Machine Translation Systems". We used 15,200 sentences parallelly aligned English-Hindi sentences. Out of this, we used 12,160 sentences for training and 3040 sentences as a tuning corpus.

For testing the MT systems, we collected 500 Arabic sentences from BBC Arabic[5] and manually translated the sentences into Hindi. The summary statistics of training, tuning, and test corpus are given in table 3.1

Language Pair	Corpus	Training	Tuning	Test
Arabic-English	UN Corpus	18,53,921	9,26,960	
Arabic-Urdu	QCRI Corpus	1,48,000	37,000	
English-Urdu	EILMT Corpus			
Urdu-English	EILMT Corpus			500
English-Hindi	EILMT Corpus	12,160	3,040	
Hindi-Urdu	EILMT Corpus			

Table 3.1: Summary Statistics of Corpus

3.2 NLP Tools

In our course of study, we used some factored MT systems. For this, we were required to use some NLP Tools. For our four languages of interest (Arabic, English, Urdu, and Hindi), we used morphological analyzers, POS taggers, and Chunkers.

For Arabic, we have used MADAMIRA[6] (Pasha et al., 2016), developed at Colombia University, for all the tasks viz morphological analysis, POS Tagging, and chunking. The POS Tagset used for this was Mada POS Tagset which was then converted into Penn Arabic Tagset. For English, we have used Stanford CoreNLP[7] (Manning et al., 2014) for all the tasks. The Tagset used, or POS tagging and chunking was Penn Tagset. For Urdu, we have used the morphological analyzer developed by Gupta et al. (2016). For POS Tagging and chunking, we have used a tagger developed by Gupta et al. (2016). The Tagset used for this was IL-POS Tagset. For Hindi, we have used Morphological Analyzer developed by Paul et al. (2013), a POS tagger developed by Joshi et al. (2013), and a chunker developed by Asopa et al. (2016). The Tagset used for this was again IL-POS Tagset.

3.3 Machine Translators Used

We used three types of translators for this research. Among these, two are toolkits, and the third is the engine developed at Banasthali Vidyapith. The first toolkit that we used was Moses MT Toolkit[8] (Koehn et al., 2007; Hoang and Koehn, 2008). We used three models for our research. These were:

1. Phrase-Based Model (PBM)
2. Factored Model using Morphological Data
3. Factored Model using POS and Chunk Data

These three models were trained for the training corpus and were improved based on the tuning corpus. For factored models, the training and tuning corpus was first prepared using the NLP tools. Table 3.2 shows the snapshot of the corpus. For readability purposes, we have used the example snapshot from the English corpus.

New|New|NNP   Horizons|Horizon|NNP   should|should|MD   be|be|VB

filling|fill|VBG   its|its|PRP$ memory|memory|NN   banks|bank|NNS

right|right|RB now|now|RB with|with|IN a|a|DT swathe|swathe|NN of|of|IN

photos|photo|NNS   and|and|CC   other|other|JJ   scientific|scientific|JJ

data|datum|NNS .|.|.

Girls|Girl|NNS are|be|VBP studying|study|VBG for|for|IN their|they|PRP$

exams|exam|NNS .|.|.

Table 3.2: Snapshot of Example Factored Corpus (English)

The second toolkit that we used was Joshua Machine Translation Toolkit[9] (Li et al., 2009). We used the hierarchical model from this toolkit. This model requires a special type of corpus to be used for training the MT engine. It used hireo grammar to convert the text into a format that is required by the toolkit. The phrase model is generated in this grammar. The snapshot of the phrase table is shown in Table 3.3.

[X] |||, jakhol [X,1] dooni |||, जखोल [X,1] दूनी||| 0 0 1 0 0 0.21889436799607423 0.14735353489371172 1 2.718 1.0 - 0.0 0 - 0.0 0 3 0

0

[X] |||, jal mahal [X,1] jantar - mantar ||| [X,1] जलमहल , जंतर – मंतर ||| 0 0 1 0 0 2.010653837224129 7.632845142924467 1 2.718 1.0 - 0.0 0 - 0.0 0 3 0 0

[X] ||| about 144 kilometers [X,1] Ranchi ||| रांची [X,1] करब 144 कलोमीटर ||| 0 0 1 0 0 1.4458368781371052 3.54569116690380837 1 2.718 1.0 - 0.0 0 - 0.0 0 4 0 0

[X] ||| if you go to this place then you ||| अगर आप इस जगह पर जाएँ तो ||| 0 0 1 0 1 9.525188187668098 18.38767053827457 1 2.718 1.0 - 0.0 0 - 0.0 0 8 0 0

Table 3.3: Snapshot of Hireo Grammar used by Joshua MT

The third MT framework used was an Example-Based Machine Translation (EBMT) which was developed at Banasthali Vidyapith (Joshi et al., 2011). For our purpose, we used two pivot languages for the translation of Arabic text into Hindi text. In all four languages were used (Arabic, English, Urdu, and Hindi). These are summarised in table 3.4.

Language No.	Language	Remark
L1	Arabic	Source Language
L2	English	Intermediate (Pivot) Language
L3	Urdu	Intermediate (Pivot) Language
L4	Hindi	Target Language

Table 3.4: Languages Used in Arabic-Hindi MT using Pivot Languages

Using these four languages a combination of MT engines was generated. These are summarised in table 3.4. In all, there were 50 MT Engines used to perform translation for Arabic to Hindi. There were four combinations of language pairs used. These were:

1. Arabic–English–Hindi (L1-L2-L4)
2. Arabic–Urdu–Hindi (L1-L3-L4)
3. Arabic–English–Urdu–Hindi (L1-L2-L3-L4)
4. Arabic–Urdu– English–Hindi (L1-L3-L2-L4)

Engine No.	Language Pairs	Remarks
E11	Arabic-English-Hindi	Translation of text from Arabic to Hindi using English as Pivot Language for Moses Phrase-Based Model
E12	Arabic-English-Hindi	Translation of text from Arabic to Hindi using English as Pivot Language for Moses Factored Model using Morphological Processing
E13	Arabic-English-Hindi	Translation of text from Arabic to Hindi using English as Pivot Language for Moses Factored Model using POS Tagging
E14	Arabic-English-Hindi	Translation of text from Arabic to Hindi using English as Pivot Language for Joshua Hierarchical Model
E15	Arabic-English-Hindi	Translation of text from Arabic to Hindi using English as Pivot Language for EBMT
E21	Arabic-Urdu-Hindi	Translation of text from Arabic to Hindi using Urdu as Pivot Language for Moses Phrase-Based Model
E22	Arabic-Urdu-Hindi	Translation of text from Arabic to Hindi using Urdu as Pivot Language for Moses Factored Model using Morphological Processing
E23	Arabic-Urdu-Hindi	Translation of text from Arabic to Hindi using Urdu as Pivot Language for Moses Factored Model using POS Tagging
E24	Arabic-Urdu-Hindi	Translation of text from Arabic to Hindi using Urdu as Pivot Language for Joshua Hierarchical Model
E25	Arabic-Urdu-Hindi	Translation of text from Arabic to Hindi using Urdu as Pivot Language for EBMT
E31	Arabic-English-Urdu-Hindi	Translation of text from Arabic to Hindi using English and Urdu as Pivot Language for Moses Phrase-Based Model
E32	Arabic-English-Urdu-Hindi	Translation of text from Arabic to Hindi using English and Urdu as Pivot Language for Moses Factored Model using Morphological Processing
E33	Arabic-English-Urdu-Hindi	Translation of text from Arabic to Hindi using English and Urdu as Pivot Language for Moses Factored Model using POS Tagging
E34	Arabic-English-Urdu-Hindi	Translation of text from Arabic to Hindi using English and Urdu as Pivot Language for Moses Factored Model using Joshua Hierarchical Model
E35	Arabic-English-Urdu-Hindi	Translation of text from Arabic to Hindi using English and Urdu as Pivot Language for EBMT
E41	Arabic-Urdu-English-Hindi	Translation of text from Arabic to Hindi using Urdu and English as Pivot Language for Moses Phrase-Based Model
E42	Arabic-Urdu-English-Hindi	Translation of text from Arabic to Hindi using Urdu and English as Pivot Language for Moses Factored Model using Morphological Processing
E43	Arabic-Urdu-English-Hindi	Translation of text from Arabic to Hindi using Urdu and English as Pivot Language for Moses Factored Model using POS Tagging

Table 3.4: MT Engines Used

Where there was just one pivot language, the source-to-target language translation has to be done using 2 MT engines. For example, doing Translation using English as a pivot language was done by translating the Arabic text into English and then translating this English text into Hindi. Where there were two pivot languages, the translation was done using 3 MT engines. For example, to perform translation from Arabic to Hindi using English and Urdu as pivot languages, the first Arabic text was translated into English using the first MT engine which was then translated into Urdu using the second MT engine. This was then translated into Hindi using the third MT engine. Thus, there were 20 MT engines that generated Hindi text.

3.4 Evaluation of Machine Translators

To identify the accuracy of the MT Engines, we performed the automatic evaluation and human evaluation. Further, we correlated the results of the two evaluation techniques. This was done on a test corpus of 500 sentences which Arabic sentences. We used a human annotator to translate these 500 sentences into Hindi manually. Further, these 500 sentences were then executed on the MT engines to get the final Hindi output which was compared with the human output. We did our evaluation using three metrics. These are described in the following section.

3.4.1 Human Evaluation

We have used an evaluation metric developed by Joshi et al. (2013) which works at the level of semantic adequacy. This is a subjective evaluation metric that takes each translation and asks a human evaluator certain questions on this translation. These questions are based on 11 parameters. They are:

1. Translation of Gender and Number of the Noun(s).
2. Identification of the Proper Noun(s).
3. Use of Adjectives and Adverbs corresponding to the Nouns and Verbs.
4. Selection of proper words/synonyms (Lexical Choice).
5. The sequence of phrases and clauses in the translation.
6. Use of Punctuation Marks in the translation.
7. Translation of tense in the sentence.
8. Translation of Voice in the sentence.
9. Maintaining the semantics of the source sentence in the translation.
10. Fluency in translated text and translator proficiency.
11. Evaluating the translation of source sentence (With respect to syntax and intended meaning).

The human evaluators were asked to give a score for each of the 11 parameters. These were on a scale of 0 to 4. Where 0 is the poor or no translation and 4 is the best or perfect translation. Finally, all the parameter's score is summed and divided into the total number of parameters used in the evaluation. This produced the objective score for this subjective evaluation. The computation of this is given in equation 3.1

$$Score = \frac{\sum_{i=1}^{n} Score\ of\ Parameter_i}{\#Parameters}$$

Equation 3.1

3.4.2 Automatic Evaluation

For automatic evaluation, we used two automatic evaluation metrics. One of the metrics works at the lexical level whereas the other metric works at the shallow semantic level. These are BLEU and Meteor respectively.

3.4.2.1 BLEU (Bilingual Evaluation Under Study): BLEU metric (2001) was used with 4-gram matching. It was used as it is considered the de-facto metric in MT evaluation. IBM proposed it in 2001. This metric matches the words produced by an MT engine with human reference translations. It judges Adequacy by looking at word matches and Fluency by looking at n-gram precision (1, 2, 3, and 4). Recall is not used in this metric. Due to this, the metric compensates it by using a brevity penalty which is calculated as the minimum between either 1 or between the division of MT output length and reference length. The final score is a weighted geometric mean of the n-gram scores. The formula is as follows:

$$BLEU = \min\left(1, \frac{MT\ output - length}{reference - length}\right) \times \exp\left(\sum_{n=1}^{N} w_n \log(p_n)\right)$$

Equation 3.2

3.4.2.2 Meteor: We used the Meteor (Metric for Evaluation of Translation with Explicit ReORdering) metric (Denkowski and Lavie, 2011) which matches translations at the shallow syntactic and semantic level. For this, the metric matches translations at a lexical level by matching lexicons, at the syntactic level by matching stems, and semantic level by matching synonyms. Further, this metric combines all the data and provides a final objective score. The scores that are computed are based on the following formulae:

$$\text{Precision} = \frac{\Sigma_i w_i \times m_i(t)}{t} \tag{3.3}$$

$$\text{Recall} = \frac{\Sigma_i w_i \times m_i(r)}{r} \tag{3.4}$$

$$F_{mean} = \frac{Precision \times Recall}{\alpha \times Precision + (1-\alpha) \times Recall} \tag{3.5}$$

$$\text{Penalty} = \gamma \times frag^{\beta} \tag{3.6}$$

$$\text{Frag} = \frac{chunks}{unigram - matches} \tag{3.7}$$

Here, at first precision and recall are calculated using equations 3.3 and 3.4. The matches are done on the bases of a beam search and lexicons, stems, and synonyms are matched to compute the numerator. Here, t refers to the MT Engine output and r refers to reference translation, w_i is the word vector which has different values for different levels. The values are shown in table 3.5.

Level	Word Vector Score
Lexical	1.0
Stem	0.8
Synonym	0.8

Table 3.5: Word Vector Values

Then F-Measure is calculated using Precision and Recall as shown in equation 3.5. With these two values, α value is also computed which is set to 0.83 for evaluation. We used three variants of the metric. Then Frag (Fragment) is calculated using equation 3.6. Here, the longest matches are termed chunks which are divided by the total no. of unigram matches found between reference translation and MT engine output. This frag score is then used to compute the penalty as shown in equation 3.7. Here with frag, γ and β values are also computed. For evaluation purposes, these are taken as 0.83 and 0.28 respectively. Finally, the score for the meteor metric is computed, as shown in equation 3.8, which is simply a product of F-Measure and Penalty.

3.6 Conclusion

In this chapter, we have explained the corpus used in our experiments. Further, we have also explained the linguistic resources, MT toolkits and MT evaluation metrics used in our research. We have also explained the development methodology and the MT systems developed in this research.

[1] https://www.udacity.com

[2] https://www.coursera.org

[3] https://www.khanacademy.org

[4] http://www/ted.com

[5] http://www.bbc.com/arabic

[6] http://www.cs.columbia.edu/~rambow/software-downloads/MADA_Distribution.html

[7] https://stanfordnlp.github.io/CoreNLP

[8] http://www.statmt.org/moses/

[9]	https://cwiki.apache.org/confluence/display/JOSHUA/Apache+Joshua+%28Incubating%29+Home

CHAPTER FOUR

Arabic-Hindi Machine Translation Using English as Pivot Language

In this chapter, we have discussed the process of translation from Arabic to Hindi via English using 5 MT engines. We have also discussed the process of evaluating the translations and the significance of these evaluations.

4.1 Design of Experiment

Among different methodologies, we wanted to study the role of English as a pivot language for the translation of text from Arabic to Hindi. Here, we used English as an intermediate language for translation. This is shown in figure 4.1.

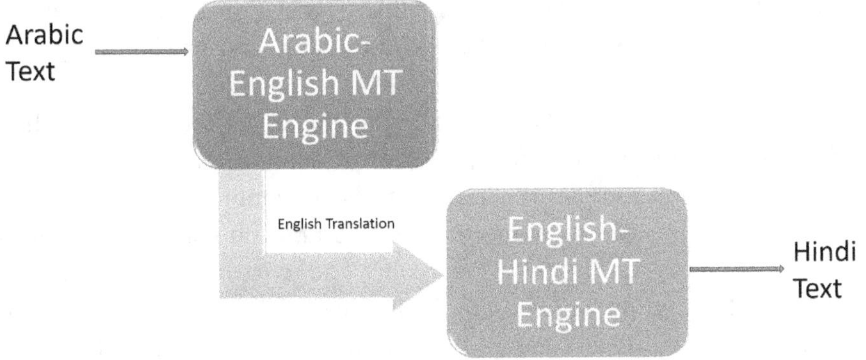

Figure 4.1: Block Diagram of Arabic-Hindi MT using English as a Pivot Language

Here, we used two MT engines, the first MT system was the Arabic-English MT system which translated Arabic text into English and the second engine was the English-Hindi MT system which translated English text into Hindi. The engines that were developed for this technique were based on the five methodologies discussed in chapter 3. Figure 4.2 shows the working of the phrase-based statistical machine translation system.

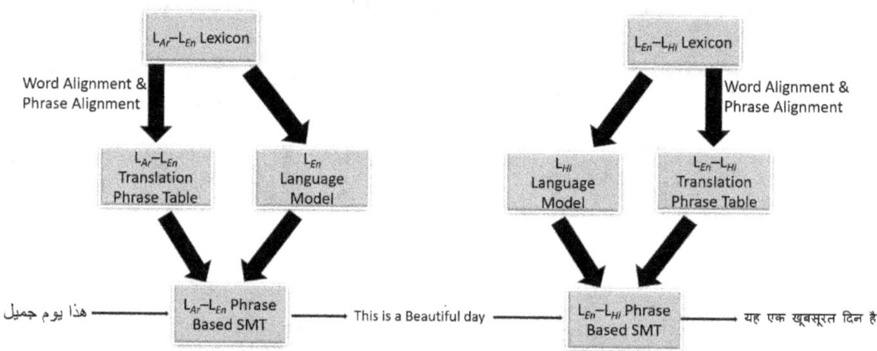

Figure 4.2: SMT System for Arabic-Hindi MT using English as a Pivot Language

Here, we have developed two SMT engines. The first engine uses Arabic-English parallel corpus to perform the translation. This takes Arabic text as input and translates it into English. The second engine uses the English-Hindi SMT engine which takes the English translation from the previous engine and sends it as input to the second engine and produces Hindi as output.

The second and third MT systems were the variations of SMT which used linguistic information for performing translations. The linguistic information that we used for this task was based on morphology and part of speech, thus the two MT systems (one based on morphological information and the other based on the part of speech.) The fourth MT system was the hierarchical MT system which used hierarchical rules to generate the target text. These systems are all broadly based on the same system architecture of SMT (with little variation) as shown in figure 4.2. The fifth MT system that we had was the EBMT system.

4.2 Evaluation Results

We evaluated our results using two popular automatic MT evaluation metrics (BLEU and Meteor) and correlated their results with human evaluation. As discussed in chapter 3, we evaluated sentence, document, and system levels. At the sentence level, we have calculated the number of times an engine produced the best translation. For BLEU, E14's translations were the best. Out of the 500 sentences, E14 had the best score in 181 sentences. The second best was E15 with 140. Table 4.1 shows the results of this study.

MT Engine	No. of Times Scored the Highest
E11	0
E12	125
E13	54
E14	181
E15	140

Table 4.1: Highest score of MT Engine for BLEU at Sentence Level for Ar-En-Hi MT

For Meteor, again E14's translations were the best. They produced the best translations on 186 instances. E15 was the second best by producing 143 translations. This is shown in figure 4.2.

MT Engine	No. of Times Scored the Highest
E11	115
E12	41
E13	15
E14	186
E15	143

Table 4.2: Highest score of MT Engine for Meteor at Sentence Level for Ar-En-Hi MT

We did the same study for Human Evaluation and found that the results do match with BLEU and Meteor. E14 produced the best translations the maximum number of times and E15 was the second best table 4.3 shows these results.

At the document level, we divided the 500 sentences into five documents of 100 sentences each and calculated the scores of each document. For BLEU, the results are shown in table 4.4. Out of the five documents, E14 had the best results in 3 documents, and E15 had the best in 2 documents. This is also shown in Figure 4.3.

MT Engine	No. of Times Scored the Highest
E11	102
E12	104
E13	47
E14	135
E15	112

Table 4.3: Highest score of MT Engine for HEval at Sentence Level for Ar-En-Hi MT

	E11	E12	E13	E14	E15
Doc1	0.375784	0.501788	0.499932	**0.552926**	0.547096
Doc2	0.338189	0.448179	0.455029	**0.507185**	0.505481
Doc3	0.363287	0.47973	0.491361	0.506252	**0.506602**
Doc4	0.358607	0.476943	0.479944	**0.533271**	0.527722
Doc5	0.361307	0.481838	0.481599	0.515314	**0.519334**

Table 4.4: Evaluation Results of BLEU on Ar-En-Hi MT at Document Level

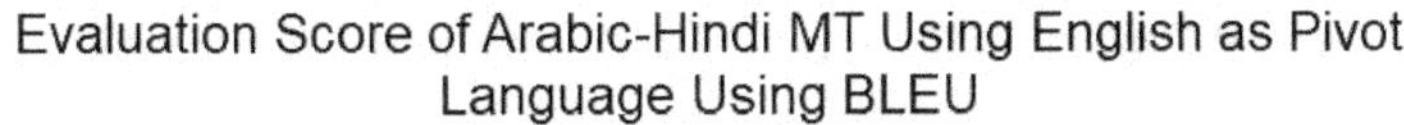

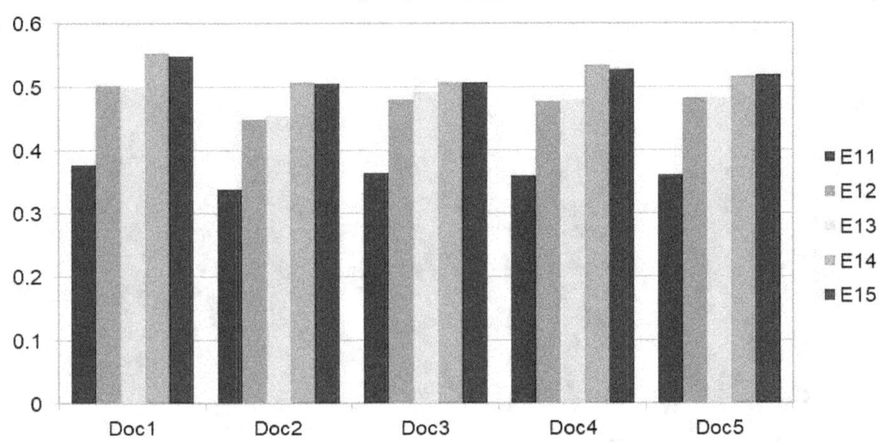

Figure 4.3: Arabic-Hindi MT Using English as Pivot Language at Document Level for BLEU

For Meteor, the results are shown in table 4.5. Here again, E14 scored the best. In 3 documents it had the highest score, and in the remaining 2, E15 had the highest score. This is also shown in figure 4.4.

	E11	E12	E13	E14	E15
Doc1	0.43325	0.3605	0.35225	**0.50825**	0.49725
Doc2	0.24225	0.162	0.1465	0.475	**0.5015**
Doc3	0.414	0.3345	0.33375	0.48325	**0.50475**
Doc4	0.49575	0.29575	0.3145	**0.5815**	0.5055
Doc5	0.61425	0.49475	0.51125	**0.692**	0.5105

Table 4.5: Evaluation Results of Meteor on Ar-En-Hi MT at Document Level

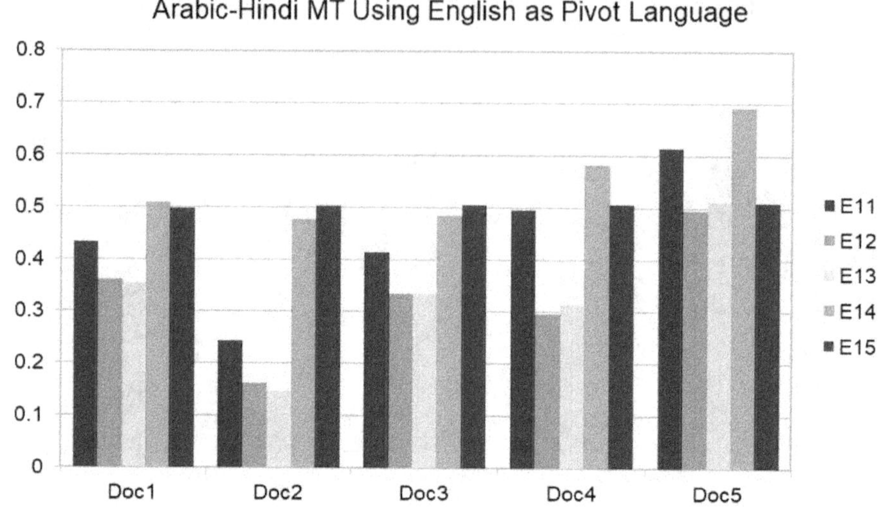

Figure 4.4: Arabic-Hindi MT Using English as Pivot Language at Document Level for Meteor

	E11	E12	E13	E14	E15
Doc1	0.501443	0.501788	0.499932	**0.552926**	0.552625
Doc2	0.394018	0.448179	0.455029	**0.507185**	0.505582
Doc3	0.333809	0.47973	0.491361	0.506252	**0.506602**
Doc4	0.428654	0.476943	0.479944	**0.533271**	0.527722
Doc5	0.456911	0.481838	0.481599	0.515314	**0.519334**

Table 4.6: Evaluation Results of HEval on Ar-En-Hi MT at Document Level

For HEval, we did the same, and the results of this evaluation are shown in table 4.6. Among the five documents, E14 again scored the best results in 3 documents and E15 scored the best in 2 documents. This is also shown in figure 4.5.

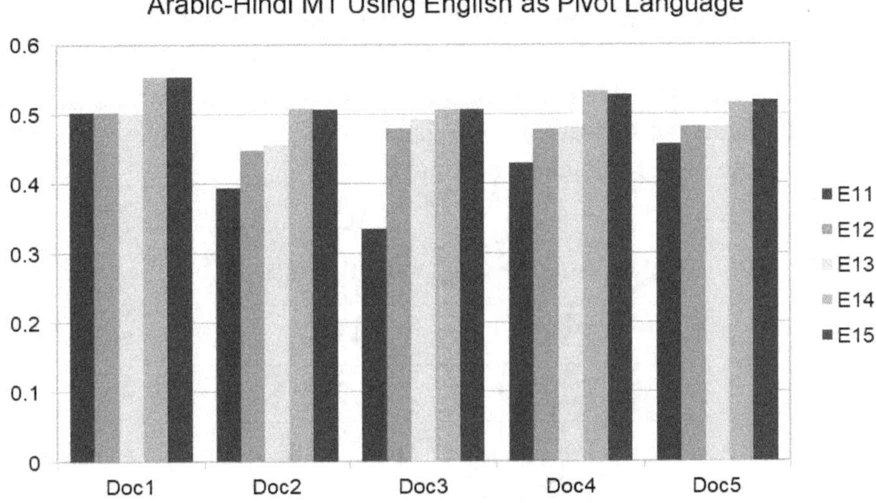

Figure 4.5: Arabic-Hindi MT Using English as Pivot Language at Document Level for HEval

Engine	System Score
E11	0.359435
E12	0.477696
E13	0.481573
E14	**0.52299**
E15	0.521247

Table 4.7: Evaluation Results of BLEU on Ar-En-Hi MT at System Level

At the system level, for BLEU, E14 scored the best results overall. For Meteor, again the best system-level score was E14. This was repeated in HEval also where again the best system-level score was E14. The result of this is shown in tables 4.7, 4.8, and 4.9 respectively. Figure 4.6 shows engine-wise scores in the system and figure 4.7 shows metric-wise scores. In both the figures, it is clearly shown that the results of all three-evaluation metrics are the same for engines E14 and E15.

Engine	System Score
E11	0.4399
E12	0.3295
E13	0.33165
E14	**0.548**
E15	0.5423

Table 4.8: Evaluation Results of Meteor on Ar-En-Hi MT at System Level

Engine	System Score
E11	0.422967
E12	0.477696
E13	0.481573
E14	**0.52299**
E15	0.522373

Table 4.9: Evaluation Results of HEval on Ar-En-Hi MT at System Level

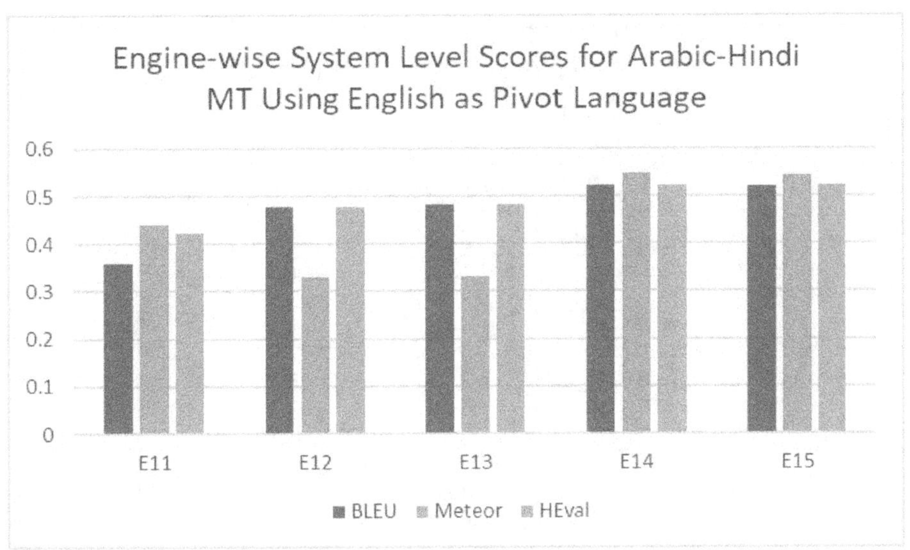

Figure 4.6: Engine-wise System Level Scores of Ar-En-Hi MT

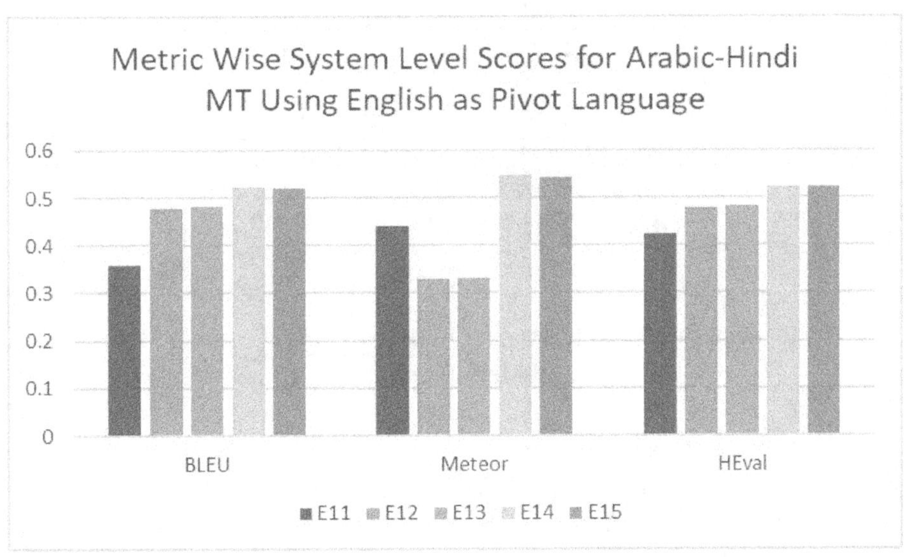

Figure 4.7: Metric-wise System Level Scores of Ar-En-Hi MT

Engine	Score
E11	0.284
E12	1.0
E13	1.0
E14	1.0
E15	0.986

Table 4.10: Pearson Correlation Between Human and BLEU Evaluation Metrics for all Engines

Engine	Score
E11	0.109
E12	0.015
E13	0.014
E14	0.024
E15	-0.027

Table 4.11: Pearson Correlation Between Human and Meteor Evaluation Metrics for all Engines

4.3 Statistical Testing

We performed statistical tests to analyze if the results were actual and did not proceed as a matter of chance. To establish this, we performed Pearson correlation where we correlated the results of the human evaluation with automatic evaluation metrics. This was done to establish that the evaluation metrics were producing the same results as that of human evaluation.

The results of the correlation between HEval and BLEU are shown in table 4.10. In all the cases the results showed a positive correlation between the two-evaluation metrics, for all the MT engines. In all the cases, except for engine E11, the correlations of BLEU with human evaluation were significant for all engines. Results of the correlation between human evaluation and Meteor automatic evaluation metric fetched low correlation. This is shown in table 5.11. Thus, we can assume that if we wish to incorporate Arabic-Hindi MT through English as a pivot language then the BLEU metric should be used for MT system development.

4.4 Conclusion

In this chapter, we showed the development of Arabic-Hindi MT using English as a pivot language. We tested the developed system through 500 sentences across levels viz. sentence, document, and system level. For this, we did both human and automatic evaluations. In the automatic evaluation, we found that BLEU was producing better results. To ascertain this, we correlated the results of BLEU with a human evaluation which is considered a golden metric. The results produced a good correlation between the two metrics. While doing the same, we found that the meteor had no or low correlation with human evaluation. Thus, we are required, can use BLEU as a de-facto metric for the development of Arabic-Hindi MT using English as the pivot language. Performance-wise, engines E14 and E15 produced the best results at all levels. Thus, we can safely say that these two engines can be used for the development of MT for this language pair using English as a pivot.

CHAPTER FIVE

Arabic-Hindi Machine Translation Using Urdu as Pivot Language

In this chapter, we have discussed the process of implementing an MT engine for Arabic-Hindi MT using Urdu as a pivot language. We believe that Urdu is closely related to Arabic and Hindi, and thus would provide better translations if we use this language as our pivot language.

5.1 Design of Experiment

Like in the previous chapter, here we have used Urdu as a pivot language. Two MT engines were used in this approach. The first performed translation of Arabic text into Urdu and the second performed the translation of Urdu-translated text into Hindi. Figure 5.1 shows the block diagram of Arabic-Hindi MT using Urdu as a pivot language.

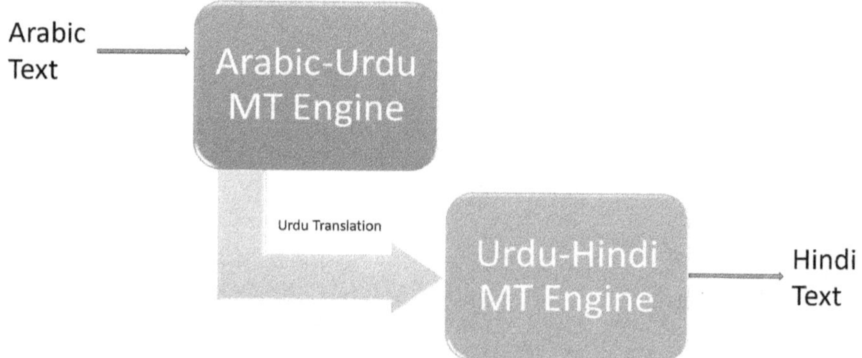

Figure 5.1: Block Diagram of Arabic-Hindi MT using Urdu as a Pivot Language

The two MT engines used parallel corpus which was used to develop translation examples for EBMT and phrase tables and language models for SMT. For the other three, it was the SMT at the core with slight modifications. Two of the three modified SMTs were based on linguistic information. One used morphological features while the other used POS-tagged data for training the model. The third modified SMT was based on hierarchical-based SMT which used an intermediate grammar for performing translations. Figure 5.2 shows the broader working of these MT engines.

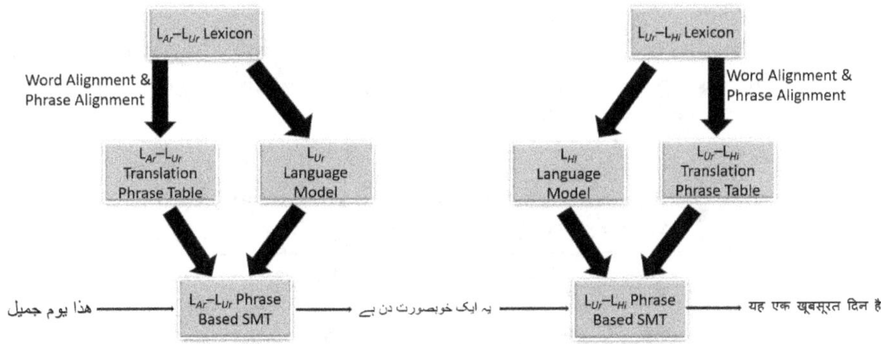

Figure 5.2: SMT engine for Arabic-Hindi MT using English as a Pivot Language

5.2 Evaluation Results

We evaluated our results using two popular automatic MT evaluation metrics and correlated their results with human evaluation. As discussed in chapter 3, we evaluated sentence, document, and system levels. As in chapter 4, we calculated the ranks of engines for each translation at the sentence level. This is shown in table 5.1. For the BLEU MT evaluation metric, here again, like for the Ar-Ur-Hi MT engine, E24 scored the best translation. It scored the best results for 422 sentences. Rest all the engines roughly scored the same best rank except for E21 which was able to produce none best translations.

MT Engine	No. of Times Scored the Highest
E21	0
E22	29
E23	15
E24	422
E25	34

Table 5.1: Highest score of MT Engine for BLEU at Sentence Level for Ar-Ur-Hi MT

For Meteor, here, E21's translations were the best. They produced the best translations on 183 instances. E24 was the second best by producing 142 translations. This is shown in table 5.2.

MT Engine	No. of Times Scored the Highest
E21	183
E22	75
E23	27
E24	142
E25	73

Table 5.2: Highest score of MT Engine for Meteor at Sentence Level for Ar-Ur-Hi MT

The same study for Human Evaluation was done. We found that the results of HEval were different from BLEU and Meteor. E24 produced the best translations the maximum number of times and E21 was the second best. Table 5.3 shows these results.

MT Engine	No. of Times Scored the Highest
E21	59
E22	17
E23	11
E24	386
E25	27

Table 5.3: Highest score of MT Engine for HEval at Sentence Level for Ar-Ur-Hi MT

At the document level, we divided 500 sentences into five documents of 100 sentences each and calculated the scores of each document. For BLEU, the results are shown in table 5.4. In all five documents, E24 had the best results This is also shown in Figure 5.3.

	E21	E22	E23	E24	E25
Doc1	0.154196	0.215052	0.19141	**0.486217**	0.290358
Doc2	0.13208	0.184148	0.164043	**0.430967**	0.234898
Doc3	0.150576	0.20893	0.188525	**0.438678**	0.25133
Doc4	0.145637	0.203611	0.180041	**0.493589**	0.26395
Doc5	0.140675	0.194285	0.17749	**0.42791**	0.229436

Table 5.4: Evaluation Results of BLEU on Ar-Ur-Hi MT at Document Level

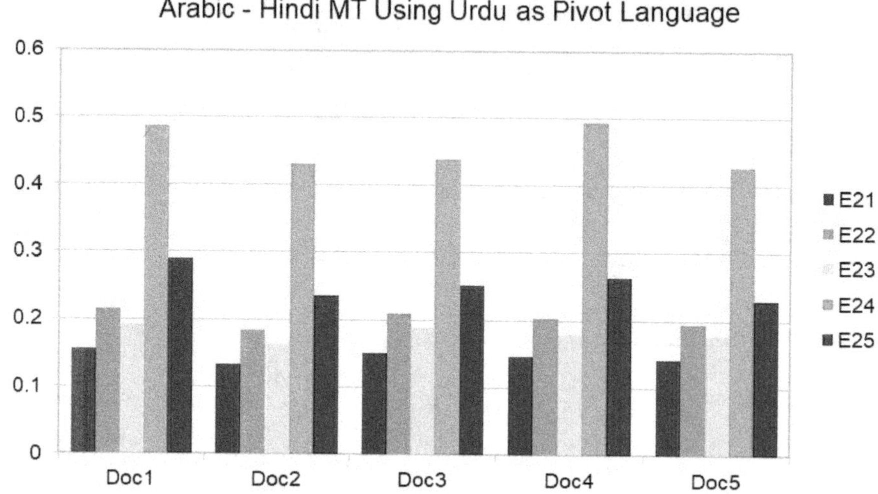

Figure 5.3: Arabic-Hindi MT Using Urdu as Pivot Language at
Document Level for BLEU

For Meteor, the results are shown in table 5.5. E21 and E24 scored the
best in 2 documents each. In 1 document, E25 had the highest score. This is
also shown in figure 5.4.

	E21	E22	E23	E24	E25
Doc1	**0.61425**	0.302	0.2545	0.38775	0.334
Doc2	0.37425	0.3855	0.33725	**0.53325**	0.2645
Doc3	**0.5665**	0.40125	0.32	0.4075	0.3405
Doc4	0.42275	0.19975	0.22725	**0.44475**	0.43225
Doc5	0.47775	0.49475	0.49475	0.3425	**0.58825**

Table 5.5: Evaluation Results of Meteor on Ar-Ur-Hi MT at Document
Level

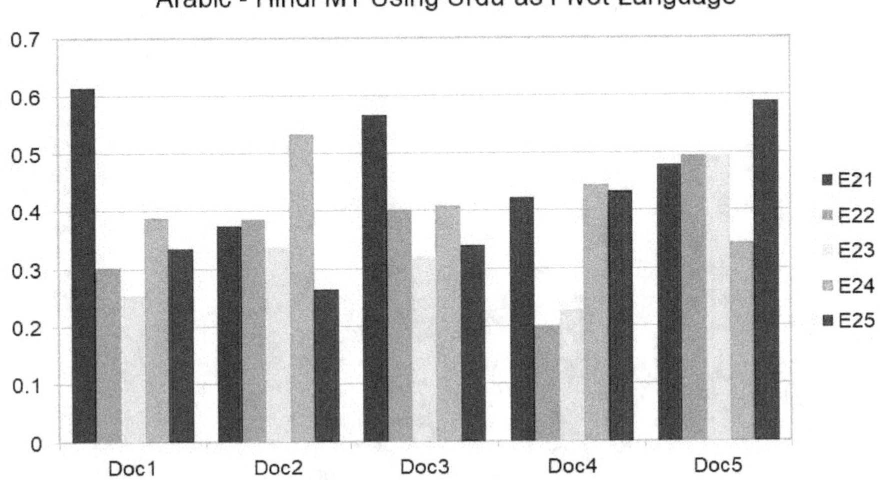

Figure 5.4: Arabic-Hindi MT Using Urdu as Pivot Language at Document Level for Meteor

	E21	E22	E23	E24	E25
Doc1	0.212452	0.215052	0.19141	**0.486217**	0.277207
Doc2	0.162512	0.184148	0.164043	**0.430967**	0.227781
Doc3	0.100894	0.20893	0.188525	**0.438678**	0.25133
Doc4	0.205436	0.203611	0.180041	**0.493589**	0.26395
Doc5	0.205996	0.194285	0.17749	**0.42791**	0.229436

Table 5.6: Evaluation Results of HEval on Ar-Ur-Hi MT at Document Level

For HEval, we did the same, and the results of this evaluation are shown in table 5.6. Among the five documents, E24 scored the best results in all documents. This is also shown in figure 5.5.

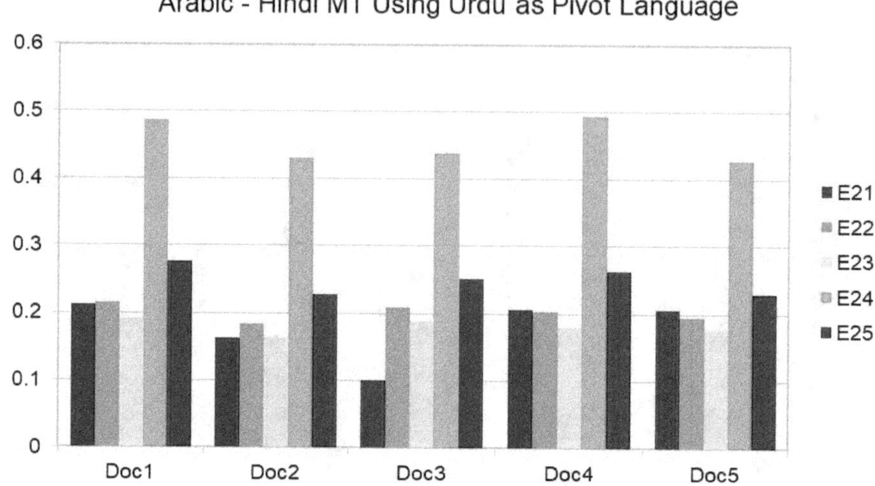

Figure 5.5: Arabic-Hindi MT Using Urdu as Pivot Language at Document Level for HEval

Engine	System Score
E21	0.144633
E22	0.201205
E23	0.180302
E24	**0.455472**
E25	0.253995

Table 5.7: Evaluation Results of BLEU on Ar-Ur-Hi MT at System Level

At the system level, for BLEU, E24 scored the best results overall. For Meteor, the best system-level score was E21. For HEval, the best system-level score was E24. The result of this is shown in tables 5.7, 5.8, and 5.9

respectively. Figure 5.6 shows the engine-wise scores of the system. Here, it is seen that meteor performed better for engines E21, E22, E23, and E25, and BLEU and HEval performed better for E24. Figure 5.7 shows metric-wise scores for BLEU and HEval, E24 scored better then rest of the MT engines and for Meteor, E21 scored better.

Engine	System Score
E21	**0.4911**
E22	0.35665
E23	0.32675
E24	0.42315
E25	0.3919

Table 5.8: Evaluation Results of Meteor on Ar-Ur-Hi MT at System Level

Engine	System Score
E21	0.177458
E22	0.201205
E23	0.180302
E24	**0.455472**
E25	0.249941

Table 5.9: Evaluation Results of HEval on Ar-Ur-Hi MT at System Level

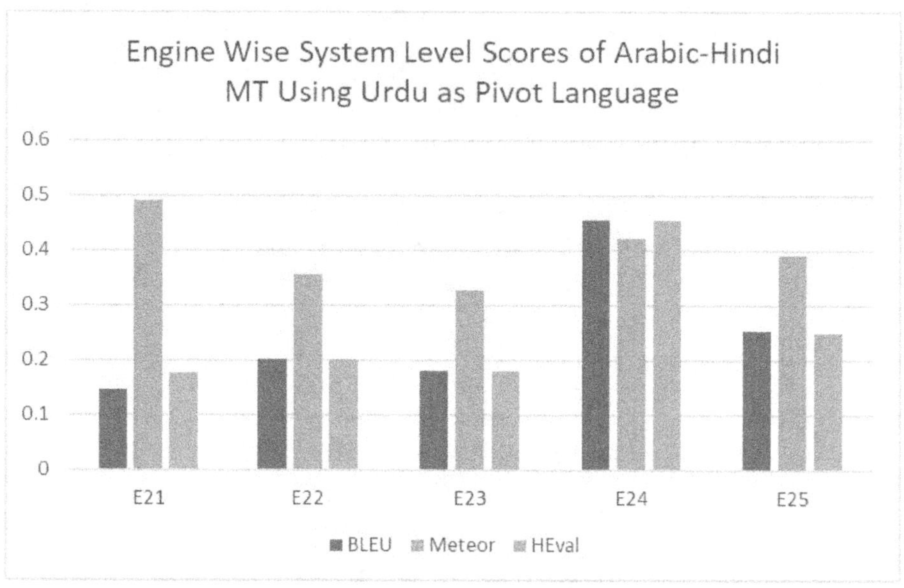

Figure 5.6: Engine-wise System Level Scores of Ar-Ur-Hi MT

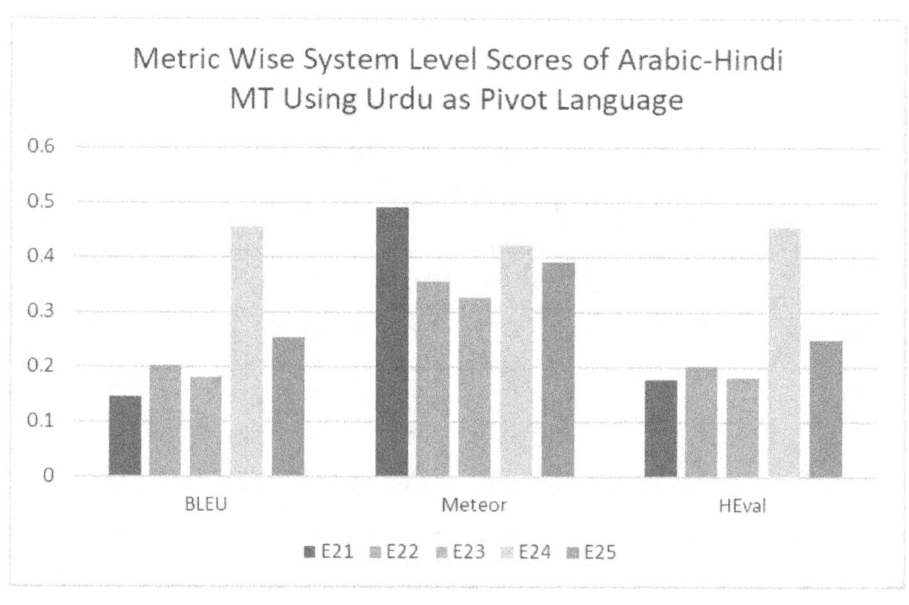

Figure 5.7: Metric-wise System Level Scores of Ar-Ur-Hi MT

Engine	Correlation Score
E21	0.2157
E22	0.2104
E23	0.2169
E24	0.2147
E25	0.2318

Table 5.10: Pearson Correlation Between Human and BLEU Evaluation Metrics for all Engines

Engine	Score
E21	-0.0046
E22	0.0277
E23	-0.0302
E24	0.0332
E25	-0.0437

Table 5.11: Pearson Correlation Between Human and Meteor Evaluation Metrics for all Engines

5.3 Statistical Testing

We performed statistical tests to analyze if the results were actual and did not proceed as a matter of chance. To establish this, we performed Pearson correlation where we correlated the results of the human evaluation with automatic evaluation metrics. This was done to establish that the evaluation metrics were producing the same results as that of human evaluation.

The results of the correlation between HEval and BLEU are shown in table 5.10. In all the cases the results showed a positive correlation between all the MT engines. In all the cases the correlations of BLEU with human evaluation were significant for all engines. Results of the correlation between human evaluation and Meteor automatic evaluation metric fetched negative or very low correlation in all cases. This is shown in table 5.11. Although the meteor's results were better than the other evaluation metrics, they did not correlate with human evaluation. Thus, we can assume that if we wish to incorporate Arabic-Hindi MT through English as a pivot language then the BLEU metric should be used for MT system development.

5.4 Conclusion

In this chapter, we showed the development of Arabic-Hindi MT using Urdu as a pivot language. We tested the developed system through 500 sentences across levels and used popular evaluation metrics for human and automatic evaluation. To ascertain if the results of automatic evaluation metrics were comparable with human evaluation metrics, we correlated their results. When BLEU was correlated with human evaluation, the results produced a good positive correlation between the two metrics. While on doing the same with meteor, we found that it produced negative and low correlations with human evaluation. Thus, if required, we can use BLEU as a de-facto metric for development of Arabic-Hindi MT using Urdu as the pivot language. Performance wise, engines E24 and E25 produced best results at all levels. There was one isolated instance where E21 performed better, but since it was with meteor which had mostly negative correlation with human evaluation, we can ignore these results. Thus, we can safely say that these two engines can be used for the development of MT for this language pair using Urdu as a pivot.

CHAPTER SIX

Arabic-Hindi Machine Translation Using Multiple Languages as Pivot Language

In this chapter, we have discussed the process of implementing an MT engine for Arabic-Hindi MT using multiple pivot languages. Here, have performed machine translation using two pivot languages. These are English and Urdu.

6.1 Design of Experiment

Here, using these languages, we incorporated two types of MT systems. The first was from Arabic to English which then used English to Urdu which then translated Urdu to Hindi. The second MT system performed translation from Arabic to Urdu which then translated Urdu translated text to English which was then translated to Hindi. The block diagram of the first MT system is shown in figure 6.1 and of the second MT system is shown in figure 6.2.

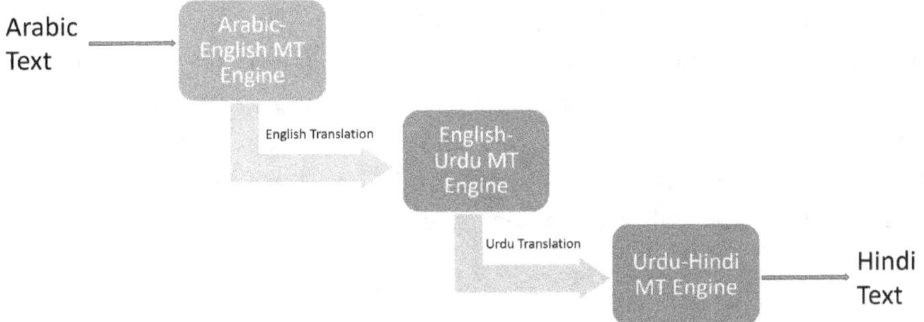

Figure 6.1: Block Diagram of Arabic-Hindi MT using English and Urdu as Pivot Languages

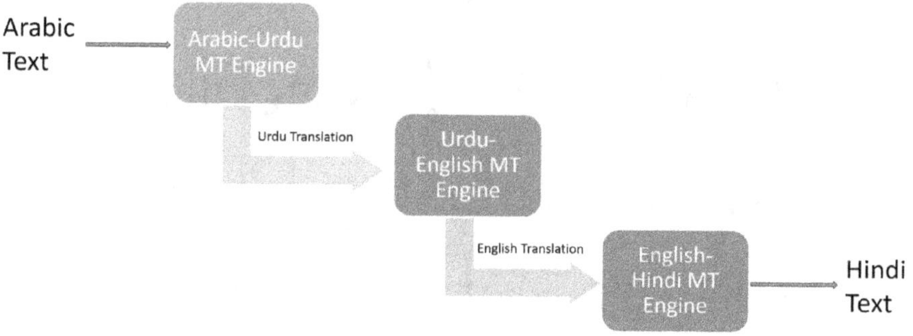

Figure 6.2: Block Diagram of Arabic-Hindi MT using Urdu and English as Pivot Languages

These MT engines used parallel corpus which was used to develop translation examples for EBMT and phrase tables and language models for SMT. For the other three, it was the SMT at the core with slight modifications. Two of the three modified SMTs were based on linguistic information. One used morphological features while the other used POS-tagged data for training the model. The third modified SMT was based on hierarchical-based SMT which used an intermediate grammar for performing translations. Figure 6.3 and 6.4 shows the broader working of these MT engines.

6.2 Evaluation Results

We evaluated our results using two popular automatic MT evaluation metrics and correlated their results with human evaluation. As discussed in chapter 3, we evaluated sentence, document, and system levels. As in the previous two chapters, we have calculated the ranks of engines for each translation at the sentence level; the same has been repeated. This is shown in tables 5.1 and 5.2 for Arabic-English-Urdu-Hindi MT System and Arabic-Urdu-English-Hindi MT system respectively.

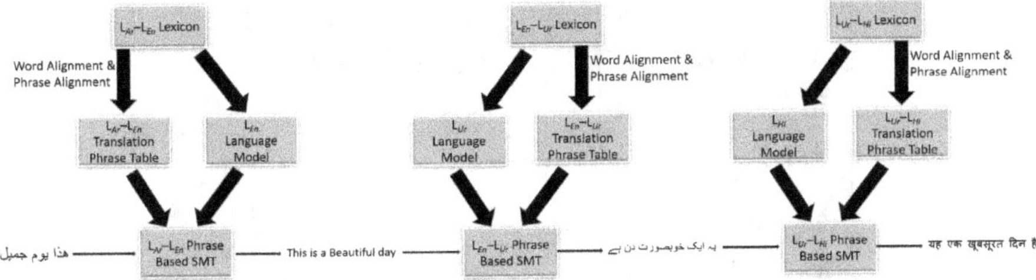

Figure 6.3: SMT System for Arabic-Hindi MT using English and Urdu as Pivot Languages

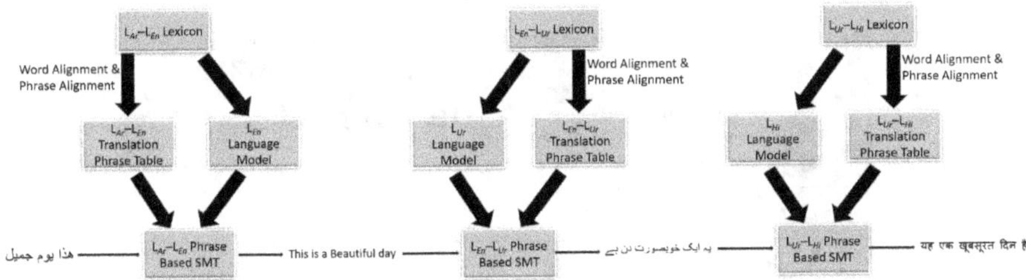

6.4: SMT System for Arabic-Hindi MT using English and Urdu as Pivot Languages

For the BLEU MT evaluation metric, in the Ar-En-Ur-Hi MT system, E34 scored the best translation in most of the cases. It scored the best results for 197 sentences. Rest all the engines roughly scored the same best rank except for E31 which was able to produce none best translations. This is shown in Table 6.1. In the Ar-Ur-En-Hi MT system, E44 produced the best translation most of the time. It produced the best translation in 214 instances. This is shown in table 6.2.

MT Engine	No. of Times Scored the Highest
E31	0
E32	97
E33	111
E34	197
E35	95

Table 6.1: Highest score of MT Engine for BLEU at Sentence Level for Ar-En-Ur-Hi MT

MT Engine	No. of Times Scored the Highest
E41	0
E42	69
E43	63
E44	214
E45	154

Table 6.2: Highest score of MT Engine for BLEU at Sentence Level for Ar-En-Ur-Hi MT

For Meteor, In Ar-En-Ur-Hi MT system, here, E34's translations were the best. They produced the best translations on 164 instances. E35 was the second best by producing 148 translations. This is shown in table 6.3. In Ar-Ur-En-Hi MT system, E44 produced the best translations with 130 instances and E45 was adjudged as the second-best MT system with 99 instances of best translations.

MT Engine	No. of Times Scored the Highest
E31	135
E32	32
E33	21
E34	164
E35	148

Table 6.3: Highest score of MT Engine for Meteor at Sentence Level for Ar-En-Ur-Hi MT

MT Engine	No. of Times Scored the Highest
E41	91
E42	94
E43	86
E44	130
E45	99

Table 6.4: Highest score of MT Engine for Meteor at Sentence Level for Ar-En-Ur-Hi MT

The same study for Human Evaluation was done. We found that the results of HEval were similar to BLEU and Meteor. In Ar-En-Ur-Hi MT system, E34 produced the best translations the maximum number of times, and E35 was the second best. Table 6.5 shows these results. In Ar-Ur-En-Hi MT system, E44 was the best MT system producing the best results with 202 instances of best translations, and E45 was the second-best with 197 instances of best translations.

MT Engine	No. of Times Scored the Highest
E41	91
E42	94
E43	86
E44	130
E45	99

Table 6.5: Highest score of MT Engine for HEval at Sentence Level for Ar-En-Ur-Hi MT

MT Engine	No. of Times Scored the Highest
E41	39
E42	51
E43	57
E44	202
E45	151

Table 6.6: Highest score of MT Engine for HEval at Sentence Level for Ar-En-Ur-Hi MT

At the document level, 500 sentences were divided into five documents of 100 sentences each. We calculated the scores of each document for the three metrics. For BLEU, In Ar-En-Ur-Hi MT System, the results are shown in table 6.7. Out of the five documents, E34 had the best results in 2 documents and E35 had the best results in 3 documents. This is also shown in Figure 6.5. In Ar-Ur-En-Hi MT System, the results are shown in table 6.8. Out of the five documents, E44 was adjudged best in 3 documents and E45 was adjudged best in 2 documents. The same is shown in figure 6.6.

	E31	E32	E33	E34	E35
Doc1	0.187185	0.246793	0.253759	0.254427	**0.277207**
Doc2	0.154893	0.202337	0.212806	**0.245839**	0.227781
Doc3	0.175801	0.236052	0.231925	0.224569	**0.25133**
Doc4	0.178267	0.231526	0.246934	**0.267011**	0.26395
Doc5	0.16375	0.216024	0.221798	0.228006	**0.229436**

Table 6.7: Evaluation Results of BLEU on Ar-En-Ur-Hi MT at Document Level

	E41	E42	E43	E44	E45
Doc1	0.125421	0.179	0.149568	**0.331375**	0.317326
Doc2	0.103708	0.144501	0.128942	0.242301	**0.24926**
Doc3	0.13515	0.187798	0.168804	**0.30489**	0.301421
Doc4	0.107971	0.154461	0.128211	**0.288361**	0.281936
Doc5	0.11922	0.163112	0.152732	0.263442	**0.275946**

Table 6.8: Evaluation Results of BLEU on Ar-Ur-En-Hi MT at Document Level

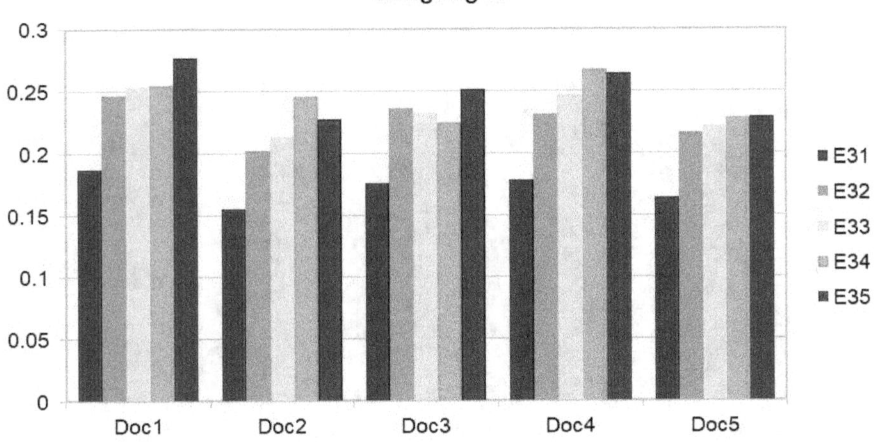

Figure 6.5: Arabic-Hindi MT Using English and Urdu as Pivot Language at Document Level for BLEU

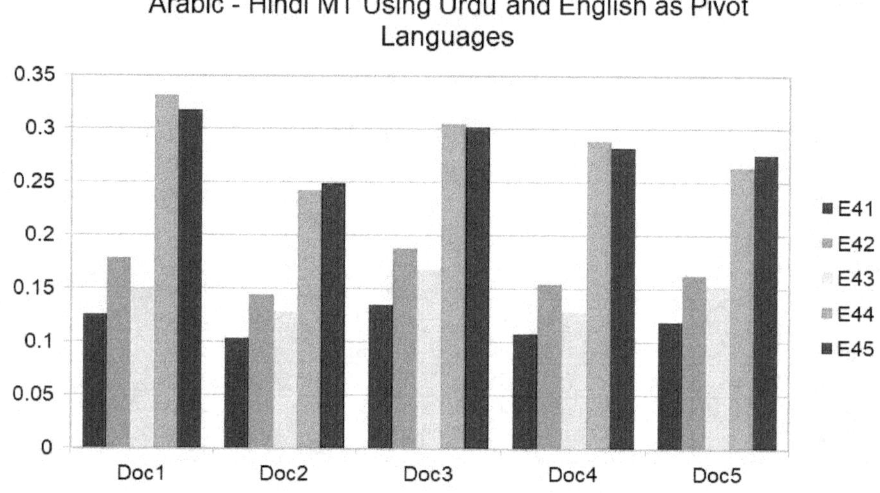

Figure 6.6: Arabic-Hindi MT Using Urdu and English as Pivot Language at Document Level for BLEU

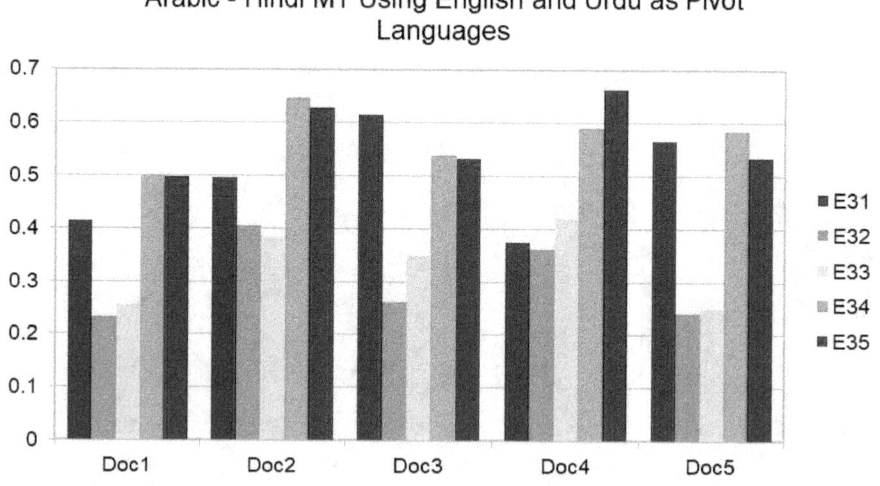

Figure 6.7: Arabic-Hindi MT Using English and Urdu as Pivot Language at Document Level for Meteor

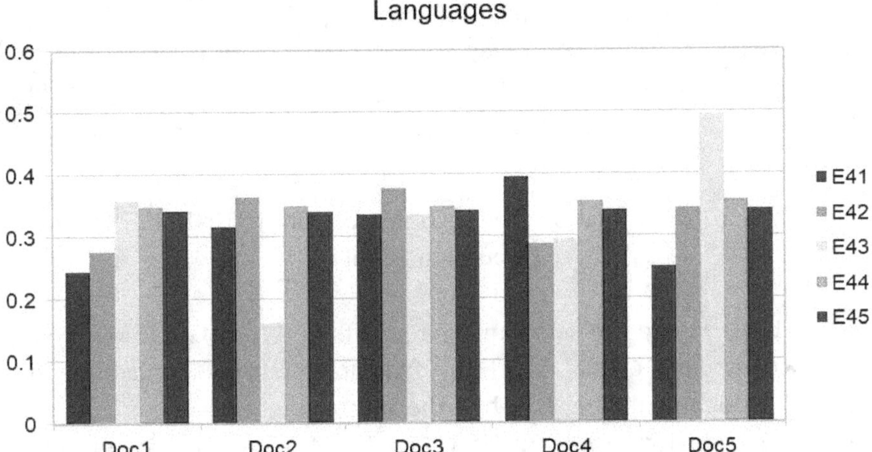

Figure 6.8: Arabic-Hindi MT Using Urdu and English as Pivot Language at Document Level for Meteor

For Meteor, In Ar-En-Ur-Hi MT System, the results are shown in table 6.9. Out of the five documents, E34 had the best results in 3 documents and E35 and E31 had the best results in 1 document each. This is also shown in Figure 6.7. In Ar-Ur-En-Hi MT System, the results are shown in table 6.8. Out of the five documents, E42 was adjudged best in 2 documents, and E41, E44, and E43 were adjudged best in 1 document each. The same is shown in figure 6.8.

	E31	E32	E33	E34	E35
Doc1	0.414	0.234	0.255	**0.49925**	0.4975
Doc2	0.49575	0.4035	0.38475	**0.64675**	0.6265
Doc3	**0.61425**	0.2605	0.349	0.539	0.5325
Doc4	0.37425	0.362	0.42175	0.591	**0.66325**
Doc5	0.5665	0.24	0.24975	**0.5855**	0.53425

Table 6.9: Evaluation Results of Meteor on Ar-En-Ur-Hi MT at Document Level

	E41	E42	E43	E44	E45
Doc1	0.2435	0.2765	0.3565	**0.34775**	0.34125
Doc2	0.31625	**0.364**	0.162	0.3485	0.34
Doc3	0.33525	**0.37825**	0.3345	0.3475	0.34175
Doc4	**0.39425**	0.28625	0.29575	0.355	0.341
Doc5	0.25075	0.34375	**0.49475**	0.35625	0.3425

Table 6.10: Evaluation Results of Meteor on Ar-Ur-En-Hi MT at Document Level

For HEval, we did the same and the results of Ar-En-Ur-Hi MT System are shown in table 6.11. Out of the five documents, E34 had the best results in 2 documents and E35 had the best results in 3 documents. This is also shown in figure 6.9. In Ar-Ur-En-Hi MT System, the results are shown in table 6.12. Out of the five documents, E44 was adjudged best in 3 documents and E45 was adjudged best in 2 documents. The same is shown in figure 6.10.

	E31	E32	E33	E34	E35
Doc1	0.254427	0.246793	0.253759	0.254427	**0.277207**
Doc2	0.245812	0.202337	0.212806	**0.245839**	0.227781
Doc3	0.224534	0.236052	0.231925	0.224569	**0.25133**
Doc4	0.265001	0.231526	0.246934	**0.267011**	0.26395
Doc5	0.215202	0.216024	0.221798	0.228006	**0.229436**

Table 6.11: Evaluation Results of HEval on Ar-En-Ur-Hi MT at Document Level

	E41	E42	E43	E44	E45
Doc1	0.1748	0.179	0.149568	**0.331375**	0.317326
Doc2	0.129199	0.144501	0.128942	0.242301	**0.24926**
Doc3	0.178488	0.187798	0.168804	**0.30489**	0.301421
Doc4	0.146756	0.154461	0.128211	**0.288361**	0.281936
Doc5	0.142289	0.163112	0.152732	0.263442	**0.275946**

Table 6.12: Evaluation Results of Meteor on Ar-Ur-En-Hi MT at Document Level

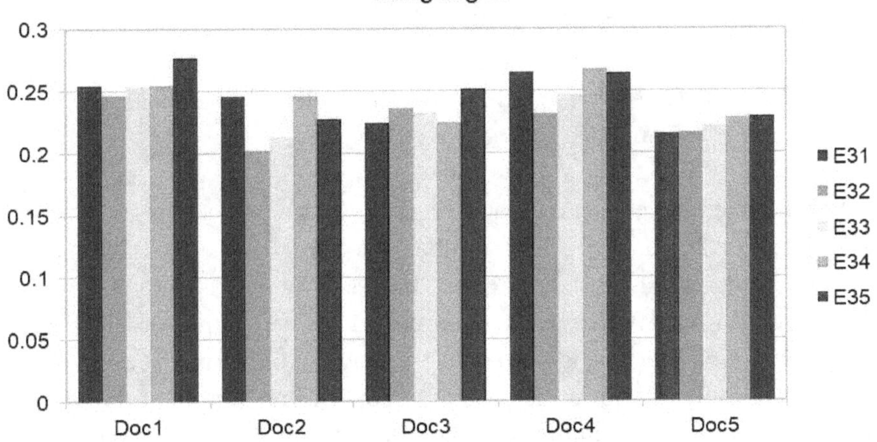

Figure 6.9: Arabic-Hindi MT Using English and Urdu as Pivot Language at Document Level for HEval

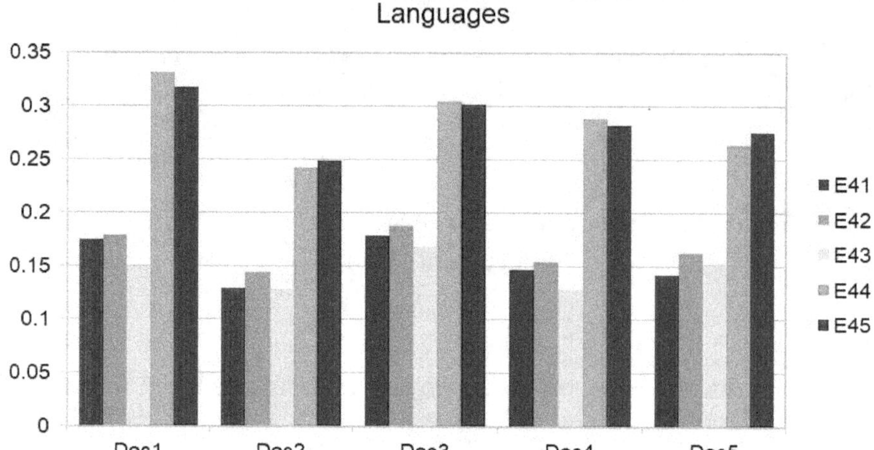

Figure 6.10: Arabic-Hindi MT Using Urdu and English as Pivot Language at Document Level for Heval

At the system level, In Ar-En-Ur-Hi, E35 scored the best results overall for BLEU. For Meteor, the best system-level score was E34. For HEval, the best system-level score was E24. The result of this is shown in tables 6.13, 6.14, and 6.15 respectively. Figure 6.11 shows engine-wise scores at the system level. Here, it is seen that the meteor performed better for all engines. Figure 6.12 shows metric-wise scores were BLEU and HEval had almost flat scores across engines and Meteor was giving better results.

Engine	System Score
E31	0.171979
E32	0.226546
E33	0.233444
E34	0.24397
E35	**0.249941**

Table 6.13: Evaluation Results of BLEU on Ar-En-Ur-Hi MT at the System Level

Engine	System Score
E31	0.49295
E32	0.3
E33	0.33205
E34	**0.5723**
E35	0.5708

Table 6.14: Evaluation Results of Meteor on Ar-En-Ur-Hi MT at System Level

Engine	System Score
E31	0.241
E32	0.2265
E33	0.2334
E34	0.244
E35	**0.2499**

Table 6.15: Evaluation Results of HEval on Ar-En-Ur-Hi MT at System Level

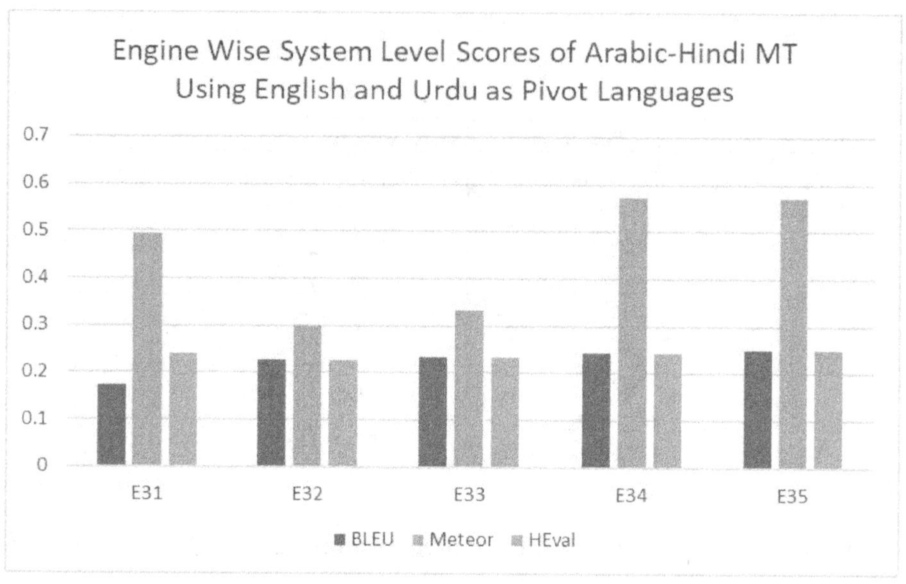

Figure 6.11: Engine-wise System Level Scores of Ar-En-Ur-Hi MT

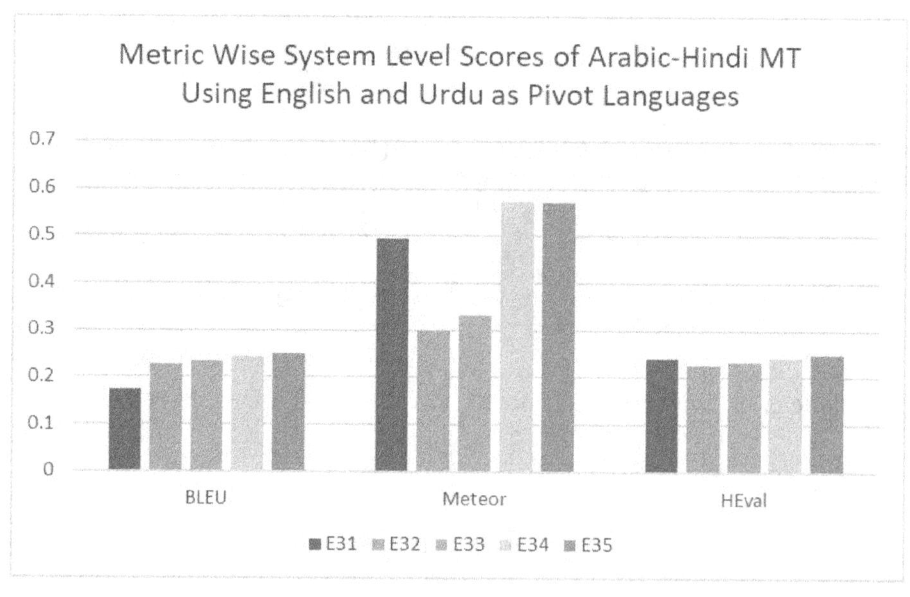

Figure 6.12: Metric-wise System Level Scores of Ar-En-Ur-Hi MT

In Ar-Ur-En-Hi, E44 scored the best results overall for BLEU. For Meteor, the best system-level score was again E44. For HEval, the best system-level score was once again E44. The result of this is shown in tables 6.16, 6.17, and 6.18 respectively. Figure 6.13 shows engine-wise scores at the system level. Here, it is seen that the meteor performed better for all engines. Figure 6.14 shows metric-wise scores where BLEU and HEval had better results for engines E44 and E45 and Meteor was giving better results overall best results for engines E44 and E45.

Engine	System Score
E41	0.118294
E42	0.165774
E43	0.145651
E44	**0.286074**
E45	0.285178

Table 6.16: Evaluation Results of BLEU on Ar-En-Ur-Hi MT at the System Level

Engine	System Score
E41	0.308
E42	0.32975
E43	0.3287
E44	**0.35375**
E45	0.34875

Table 6.17: Evaluation Results of Meteor on Ar-En-Ur-Hi MT at System Level

Engine	System Score
E41	0.154306
E42	0.165774
E43	0.145651
E44	**0.286074**
E45	0.285178

Table 6.18: Evaluation Results of HEval on Ar-En-Ur-Hi MT at System Level

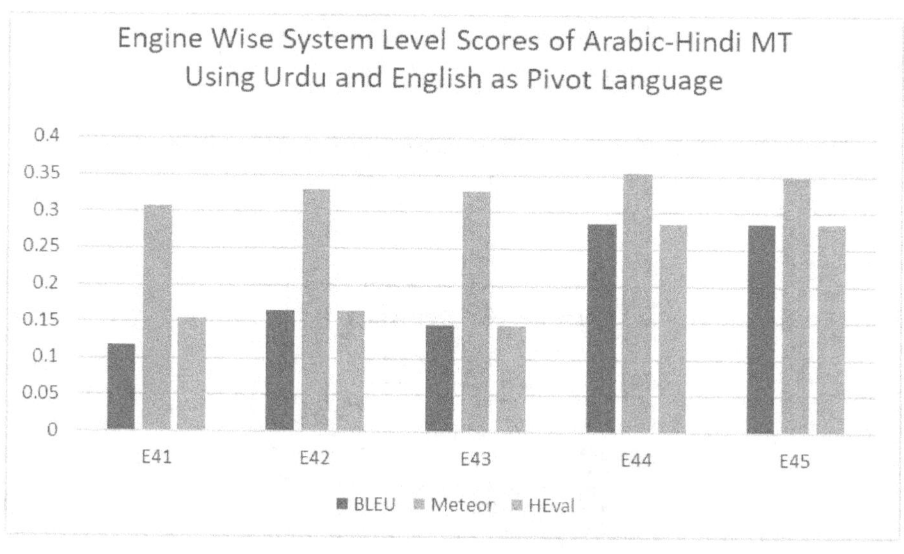

Figure 6.13: Engine-wise System Level Scores of Ar-Ur-En-Hi MT

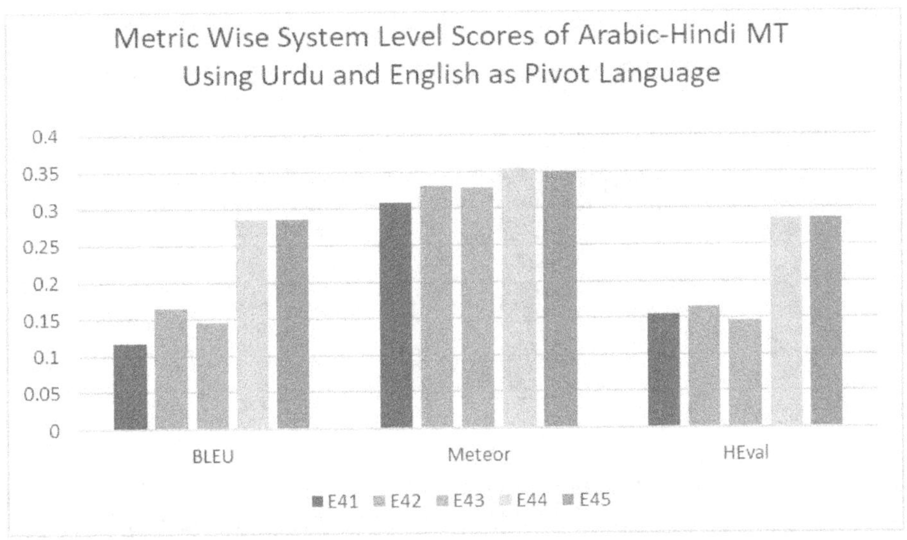

Figure 6.14: Metric-wise System Level Scores of Ar-Ur-En-Hi MT

5.3 Statistical Testing

For Ar-En-Ur-Hi MT system, the results of the correlation between HEval and BLEU are shown in table 6.19. In all the cases the results showed a positive correlation between all the MT engines. In all the cases the correlations of BLEU with human evaluation were significant for all engines. Results of the correlation between human evaluation and Meteor automatic evaluation metric again fetched negative or very low correlation in all cases. This is shown in table 6.20. Thus, we can again assume that if we wish to incorporate Arabic-Hindi MT through English and Urdu as two pivot languages then the BLEU metric should be used for MT system development.

Engine	Correlation Score
E31	0.0985
E32	0.1363
E33	0.1088
E34	0.1854
E35	0.2318

Table 6.19: Pearson Correlation Between Human and BLEU Evaluation Metrics Across all Engines for English and Urdu as Pivot Languages

Engine	Score
E31	-0.0046
E32	0.0277
E33	-0.0302
E34	0.0332
E35	-0.0437

Table 6.20: Pearson Correlation Between Human and Meteor Evaluation Metrics Across all Engines for English and Urdu as Pivot Languages

For Ar-Ur-En-Hi MT system, the results of the correlation between HEval and BLEU are shown in table 6.21. As always, in all the cases the results showed a high positive correlation between all the MT engines. In all the cases the correlations of BLEU with human evaluation were significant for all engines. Results of the correlation between human evaluation and Meteor automatic evaluation metric again fetched negative correlations in all cases. This is shown in table 6.22. Thus, we can assume that if we wish to incorporate Arabic-Hindi MT through Urdu and English as two pivot languages then the BLEU metric should be used for MT system development.

Engine	Correlation Score
E41	0.8768
E42	1
E43	1
E44	1
E45	1

Table 6.21: Pearson Correlation Between Human and BLEU Evaluation Metrics Across all Engines for Urdu and English as Pivot Languages

Engine	Score
E41	-0.0226
E42	0.0756
E43	-0.0005
E44	-0.0163
E45	0.0297

Table 6.22: Pearson Correlation Between Human and Meteor Evaluation Metrics Across all Engines for Urdu and English as Pivot Languages

6.4 Conclusion

In this chapter, we showed the development of Arabic-Hindi MT using multiple pivot languages. Here we used English and Urdu as pivot languages. While using the combination of English and Urdu, Arabic was translated into English which was then translated into Urdu and finally into Hindi, the results of the correlation between BLEU and human evaluation fetched a good positive correlation between the two metrics. While doing the same with meteor, we found that it produced negative and low correlations with human evaluation. The same was the case when with used Urdu as the first pivot language and English as the second pivot language. Thus, if required, we can use BLEU as a de-facto metric for the development of Arabic-Hindi MT using English and Urdu as pivot languages. Performance-wise, For Ar-En-Ur-Hi MT system, there were no engines that could produce the best results. E33 and E34 did produce the best results with meteor, but since they had a negative correlation with the human evaluation metric, we cannot consider their results. Thus, for this combination of pivot languages, we cannot say, which approach would produce better results. For Ar-Ur-En-Hi MT system, E44 and E45 produced the best results with all three metrics. Thus, in case we wish to use English and Urdu as two pivot languages for developing the Arabic-Hindi MT system, then Urdu should be used as the first pivot language and English should be used as the second pivot language.

Moreover, we can MT engines which are based on E44 and E45 mechanisms for this purpose.

CHAPTER SEVEN

Epilogue

In this book, we have studied the development and evaluation of the Arabic-Hindi MT system using the pivot approach. For this purpose, we have used English and Urdu as pivot languages. For our study, we have developed several MT engines for 4 MT systems. The first MT system was Arabic-Hindi MT using English as a pivot language. It had 2 MT engines. The first MT engine translated Arabic text into English and the second MT engine translated English translated text into Hindi. The second MT system also had 2 MT engines. Here instead of English, we used Urdu. Thus, the Arabic text was translated into Urdu by the first MT engine, and then this Urdu translation was translated into Hindi by the second MT engine. The third MT system had 3 MT engines and two pivot languages. The first MT engine translated Arabic text into English then this English was translated into Urdu via the second MT engine which was then finally translated into Hindi using the third MT engine. The fourth MT system again had 3 MT engines with two pivot languages. Here Arabic was first translated into Urdu using the first MT engine which was then translated into English using a second MT engine and finally was translated into Hindi using the third MT engine. In this chapter, we have shared the finding of this research.

7.1 Experimental Setup

Since we did not have a parallel corpus for the Arabic-Hindi language pair. We employed the pivot-based approach for the translation of Arabic into Hindi. For this, we used English and Urdu as pivot languages. For implementing the Arabic-English MT system, we have used UN corpus, for Arabic-Urdu we have used QCRI corpus developed by Qatar Computing Research Institute. For English-Hindi, Urdu-Hindi, English-Urdu, and Urdu-English language pairs, we have used the EILMT corpus.

For our research, we have developed multiple MT engines using different mechanisms. The first was the baseline system which was based on the statistical MT approach. This was the simple phrase-based SMT. The next two MT engines were the modifications of this plain vanilla MT system. They used linguistic information for performance improvement. The first MT used morphological information and the second used POS tags. For this, we need morphology and POS-based linguistic tools for all the languages used in our study. For Arabic, we have used two developed at Columbia University. For English, we have used Stanford CoreNLP for morphological analysis and POS tagging. For Urdu and Hindi, we have used the tools developed at Banasthali Vidyapith. The fourth MT system was based on hierarchical PBMT, and the fifth MT mechanism was based on an example-based approach. To ascertain, whether the translations were good or not, we employed human and automatic evaluation metrics. For human evaluation, we have used the HEval metric which works at a semantic adequacy level, and for automatic evaluation, we have used BLEU and Meteor which are one of the most popular automatic MT evaluation metrics.

7.2 Arabic-Hindi MT using English as Pivot Language

While using English as a pivot language for Arabic-Hindi MT, we have developed 5 MT systems using 2 MT engines each. The outputs of MT engines were evaluated by HEval, a human evaluation metric, and BLEU and Meteor which were automatic evaluation metrics. The results of the MT system which was based on Hierarchical PBMT were better than the other approaches. The example-based MT system produced the second-best results. Here, BLEU provided better correlations with HEval than Meteor. Thus, while developing the MT system using this pivot pair, we can use the BLEU MT evaluation metric for the MT system development process.

7.3 Arabic-Hindi MT using Urdu as Pivot Language

While using Urdu as a pivot language for Arabic-Hindi MT. The results of the MT system which was based on Hierarchical PBMT were again better than the other approaches. The second-best results were again produced by an example-based MT system. Here, BLEU again provided better correlations with HEval than Meteor. Thus, while developing the MT system using this pivot pair, we can use the BLEU MT evaluation metric for the MT system development process. Although, the results of using English as a pivot language and Urdu as a pivot language were similar. The output of the MT system which used English as the pivot language produced better translations than the system which used Urdu as the pivot language. Thus, if we have a choice of selecting a pivot language between Arabic and Urdu, we should choose English over Urdu. One possible reason for this could be the size of the corpus used to develop the two MT systems. Arabic-English corpus was much larger than the Arabic-Urdu corpus.

7.4 Arabic-Hindi MT using English and Urdu as Pivot Languages

While using English and Urdu as a pivot language for Arabic-Hindi MT. No MT system was able to produce better results. The result of all the MT systems was the same. Thus, we cannot identify any better MT system for this pair of pivot languages.

7.5 Arabic-Hindi MT using Urdu and English as Pivot Languages

While using Urdu English as a pivot language for Arabic-Hindi MT. Again, hierarchical phrase-based MT was best and the example-based approach was second best. On comparing the result of this MT system with the ones that had English and Urdu as pivot languages, the result of these systems was better. On comparing the results of these systems with all other MT systems, it was found that the ones which had English as the only pivot language produced better results. Here again, BLEU produced a better correlation with human evaluation.

7.6 Future Directions

Since, in all the cases, Hierarchical phrase-based MT produced the best results, and this approach used herio grammar for training the MT system. It would be interesting to see the results of the MT system developed using a transfer-based approach. Its comparison with the best approaches in this study can be one possible extension of this study.

Another, possible future study can be the one in which we enhance our training corpus which is Urdu as one of the languages (For Arabic-Urdu, English-Urdu, and Urdu-Hindi language pairs). In our research, the use of Urdu fetched very promising results. Due to the lack of availability of a large corpus, the system could not perform better. Maybe if we have a good size corpus, we may improve the outputs of the system which has used Urdu as the pivot language.

One more extension to this study could be the incorporation of a neural-based MT system (NMT). In the past 2-3 years, the use of NMT has increased. NMT has started to show promising results, provided it has a very good clean corpus. If not, the results show that the system's performance degrades drastically. So another study can use a hybrid model for translation using any of the MT mechanisms used in our study with NMT.

References

Abdelali, A., Guzman, F., Sajjad, H., & Vogel, S. 2014. "The AMARA Corpus: Building Parallel Language Resources for the Educational Domain". In LREC Vol. 14.

Ács, J., 2014. Pivot-based multilingual dictionary building using wiktionary.

Acs, J., Pajkossy, K. and Kornai, A., 2013. Building basic vocabulary across 40 languages. In Proceedings of the sixth workshop on building and using comparable corpora (pp. 52-58).

Aker, A., Paramita, M.L., Pinnis, M. and Gaizauskas, R., 2014, May. Bilingual dictionaries for all EU languages. In LREC 2014 Proceedings (pp. 2839-2845). European Language Resources Association.

Al-Hunaity, M., Maegaard, B. and Hansen, D., 2010. Using English as a pivot language to enhance Danish-Arabic statistical machine translation. In Proc. of LREC 2010: Workshop on Language Resources and Human Language Technology for Semitic Languages (pp. 108-113).

Arfath Pasha, Mohamed Al-Badrashiny, Mona Diab, Ahmed El Kholy, Ramy Eskander, Nizar Habash, Manoj Pooleery, Owen Rambow, and Ryan M. Roth. 2016. "MADAMIRA: A Fast, Comprehensive Tool for Morphological Analysis and Disambiguation of Arabic." LREC. Vol. 14.

Arka, I.W., 2002. Voice systems in the Austronesian languages of Nusantara: Typology, symmetricality and Undergoer orientation.

Asopa, S., Asopa, P., Mathur, I., & Joshi, N. 2016. "Rule based chunker for Hindi." Contemporary Computing and Informatics (IC3I), 2016 2nd International Conference on. IEEE.

Babych, B., Hartley, A. and Sharoff, S., 2007. Translating from under-resourced languages: comparing direct transfer against pivot translation. Proceedings of the MT Summit XI, pp.412-418.

Bakhshaei, S., Safabakhsh, R. and Khadivi, S., 2019. Extracting parallel fragments from comparable documents using a generative model. Computer Speech & Language, 53, pp.25-42.

Ballesteros, L. and Sanderson, M., 2003, November. Addressing the lack of direct translation resources for cross-language retrieval. In Proceedings of the twelfth international conference on Information and knowledge management (pp. 147-152). ACM.

Bertoldi, N., Barbaiani, M., Federico, M. and Cattoni, R., 2008. Phrase-based statistical machine translation with pivot languages. In International Workshop on Spoken Language Translation (IWSLT) 2008.

Blelloch, G.E. and Sabot, G.W., 1990. Compiling collection-oriented languages onto massively parallel computers. Journal of parallel and distributed computing, 8(2), pp.119-134.

Boitet, C. and Tsai, W.J., 2002. Coedition to share text revision across languages. Proc. COLING-02 WS on MT, Taipeh, p.8.

Boitet, C., 2001. Four technical and organizational keys for handling more languages and improving quality (on demand) in MT. In Proc. MTS2001 Workshop on" MT2010—Towards a Road Map for MT", Santiago de Compostela (Vol. 18, No. 9, p. 01).

Bond, F., Sulong, R., Yamazaki, T. and Ogura, K., 2001. Design and construction of a machine-tractable Japanese-Malay dictionary.

Borin, L., 2000a, July. You'll take the high road and I'll take the low road: using a third language to improve bilingual word alignment. In Proceedings of the 18th conference on Computational linguistics-Volume 1 (pp. 97-103). Association for Computational Linguistics.

Borin, L., 2000b. Pivot alignment. In Proceedings of the 12th Nordic Conference of Computational Linguistics (NODALIDA 1999) (pp. 41-48).

Bräuer, M. and Demuth, B., 2007, September. Model-level integration of the OCL standard library using a pivot model with generics support. In International Conference on Model Driven Engineering Languages and Systems (pp. 182-193). Springer, Berlin, Heidelberg.

Cettolo, M., Bertoldi, N. and Federico, M., 2011. Bootstrapping Arabic-Italian SMT through comparable texts and pivot translation. In 15th Annual Conference of the European Association for Machine Translation (EAMT).

Cheng, Y., Yang, Q., Liu, Y., Sun, M. and Xu, W., 2017, August. Joint training for pivot-based neural machine translation. In Proceedings of IJCAI.

Christy, S., WordStream Inc, 2002. Translation and communication of a digital message using a pivot language. U.S. Patent Application 09/820,153.

Costa-Jussà, M.R., Henríquez, C. and Banchs, R.E., 2011. Enhancing scarce-resource language translation through pivot combinations. In Proceedings of 5th International Joint Conference on Natural Language Processing (pp. 1361-1365).

Creutz, M., 2018. Open Subtitles Paraphrase Corpus for Six Languages. arXiv preprint arXiv:1809.06142.

Dabre, R., Cromieres, F., Kurohashi, S. and Bhattacharyya, P., 2015. Leveraging small multilingual corpora for smt using many pivot languages. In Proceedings of the 2015 Conference of the North American Chapter of the Association for Computational Linguistics: Human Language Technologies (pp. 1192-1202).

Dahlmeier, D., Liu, C. and Ng, H.T., 2011, July. Tesla at wmt 2011: Translation evaluation and tunable metric. In Proceedings of the Sixth Workshop on Statistical Machine Translation (pp. 78-84). Association for Computational Linguistics.

Darlington, J., Guo, Y., To, H. W., Wu, Q., Yang, J., & Kohler, M. (1994, November). Fortran-S: a uniform functional interface to parallel imperative languages. In Proceedings of the Third Parallel Computing Workshop, Fujitsu Laboratories Ltd, Kawasaki Japan.

David, P., 1994. Using pivot consistency to decompose and solve functional CSPs. Journal of Artificial Intelligence Research, 2, pp.447-474.

Dayley, J.P., 1983. Voice and ergativity in Mayan languages.

Denkowski, M. and Lavie, A. 2011. Meteor 1.3: Automatic Metric for Reliable Optimization and Evaluation of Machine Translation Systems. In Proceedings of the EMNLP 2011 Workshop on Statistical Machine Translation, 2011

Dholakia, R. and Sarkar, A., 2014. Pivot-based triangulation for low-resource languages. In Proc. AMTA (pp. 315-328).

Di Ruscio, D., Malavolta, I., Muccini, H., Pelliccione, P. and Pierantonio, A., 2012, March. Model-driven techniques to enhance architectural languages interoperability. In International Conference on Fundamental Approaches to Software Engineering (pp. 26-42). Springer, Berlin, Heidelberg.

El Kholy, A. and Habash, N., 2014. Alignment symmetrization optimization targeting phrase pivot statistical machine translation. Proceedings of The European Association for Machine Translation (EAMT14).

El Kholy, A., Habash, N., Leusch, G., Matusov, E. and Sawaf, H., 2013a. Language independent connectivity strength features for phrase pivot statistical machine translation. In Proceedings of the 51st Annual Meeting of the Association for Computational Linguistics (Volume 2: Short Papers) (Vol. 2, pp. 412-418).

El Kholy, A., Habash, N., Leusch, G., Matusov, E. and Sawaf, H., 2013b. Selective combination of pivot and direct statistical machine translation models. In Proceedings of the Sixth International Joint Conference on Natural Language Processing (pp. 1174-1180).

Euzenat, J., and Stucken Schmidt, H., 2003. The 'family of languages' approach to semantic interoperability. Knowledge transformation for the semantic web, 95, p.49.

Gey, F.C., 2000, September. Research to Improve Cross-Language Retrieval—Position Paper for CLEF. In Workshop of the Cross-Language Evaluation Forum for European Languages (pp. 83-88). Springer, Berlin, Heidelberg.

Gollins, T. and Sanderson, M., 2001, September. Improving cross language retrieval with triangulated translation. In Proceedings of the 24th annual international ACM SIGIR conference on Research and development in information retrieval (pp. 90-95). ACM.

Gupta, V., Joshi, N., & Mathur, I. 2016. "Design and development of a rule-based Urdu lemmatizer". In Proceedings of International Conference on ICT for Sustainable Development (pp. 161-169). Springer, Singapore.

Gupta, V., Joshi, N., & Mathur, I. 2016. "POS tagger for Urdu using Stochastic approaches." Proceedings of the Second International Conference on Information and Communication Technology for Competitive Strategies. ACM.

Habash, N. and Hu, J., 2009, March. Improving Arabic-Chinese statistical machine translation using English as pivot language. In Proceedings of the Fourth Workshop on Statistical Machine Translation (pp. 173-181). Association for Computational Linguistics.

Hajič, J., Hric, J. and Kuboň, V., 2000, April. Machine translation of very close languages. In Proceedings of the sixth conference on Applied natural language processing (pp. 7-12). Association for Computational Linguistics.

Heidenreich, F., Johannes, J., Karol, S., Seifert, M., Thiele, M., Wende, C. and Wilke, C., 2010, October. Integrating OCL and textual modelling languages. In International Conference on Model Driven Engineering Languages and Systems (pp. 349-363). Springer, Berlin, Heidelberg.

Hermann, K.M. and Blunsom, P., 2013. Multilingual distributed representations without word alignment. arXiv preprint arXiv:1312.6173.

Hoang, H. and Koehn, P., 2008. "Design of the moses decoder for statistical machine translation." In Software Engineering, Testing, and Quality Assurance for Natural Language Processing (pp. 58-65). Association for Computational Linguistics.

Homola, P. and Kubon, V., 2004. A translation model for languages of acceding countries. In Proceedings of the EAMT Workshop, Malta.

Hutchins, J. 2005. The first public demonstration of machine translation: the Georgetown-IBM system, 7th January 1954. Publicación electrónica en: http://www. hutchinsweb. me. uk/GUIBM-2005. pdf.

Joshi, N. Mathur, M. Darbari, H. Kumar, A. 2013, HEval: Yet Another Human Evaluation Metric, International Journal of Natural Language Computing, pp 21-36, Vol 2(5).

Joshi, N., Darbari, H. & Mathur, I. 2013. "HMM based POS tagger for Hindi." Proceeding of 2013 International Conference on Artificial Intelligence, Soft Computing (AISC-2013).

Joshi, N., Mathur, I. and Mathur, S., 2011, February. "Translation memory for indian languages: an aid for human translators." In Proceedings of the International Conference & Workshop on Emerging Trends in Technology (pp. 711-714). ACM.

Kholy, A.E. and Habash, N., 2016. Morphological Constraints for Phrase Pivot Statistical Machine Translation. arXiv preprint arXiv:1609.03376.

Kim, J.H., Seo, H.W. and Kwon, H.S., 2013. Bilingual lexicon induction through a pivot language. Journal of the Korean Society of Marine Engineering, 37(3), pp.300-306.

Kishida, K. and Kando, N., 2003, August. Two-stage refinement of query translation in a pivot language approach to cross-lingual information retrieval: An experiment at CLEF 2003. In Workshop of the Cross-Language Evaluation Forum for European Languages (pp. 253-262). Springer, Berlin, Heidelberg.

Koehn, P. and Monz, C., 2005, June. Shared task: Statistical machine translation between European languages. In Proceedings of the ACL Workshop on Building and Using Parallel Texts (pp. 119-124). Association for Computational Linguistics.

Koehn, P., Birch, A. and Steinberger, R., 2009. 462 machine translation systems for europe. Proceedings of MT Summit XII, pp.65-72.

Koehn, P., Hoang, H., Birch, A., Callison-Burch, C., Federico, M., Bertoldi, N., Cowan, B., Shen, W., Moran, C., Zens, R. and Dyer, C. 2007. "Moses: Open source toolkit for statistical machine translation." In Proceedings of the 45th annual meeting of the ACL on interactive poster and demonstration sessions (pp. 177-180). Association for Computational Linguistics.

Kwon, H.S., Seo, H.W. and Kim, J.H., 2013. Bilingual lexicon extraction via pivot language and word alignment tool. In Proceedings of the Sixth Workshop on Building and Using Comparable Corpora (pp. 11-15).

Lata, S. and Somnath, C. V. K. (2010). Development of Linguistic Resources and Tools for Providing Multilingual Solutions in Indian Languages - A Report on National Initiative, In Proceedings of the Seventh International Conference on Language Resources and Evaluation (LREC'10), Valletta, Malta.

Lee, L., 1996. Learning of context-free languages: A survey of the literature.

Lehtokangas, R. and Airio, E., 2002, August. Translation via a pivot language challenges direct translation in CLIR. In Proceedings of the SIGIR 2002 Workshop: Cross-Language Information Retrieval: A Research Roadmap.

Leusch, G., Max, A., Crego, J.M. and Ney, H., 2010. Multi-pivot translation by system combination. In International Workshop on Spoken Language Translation (IWSLT) 2010.

Li, Z., Callison-Burch, C., Dyer, C., Ganitkevitch, J., Khudanpur, S., Schwartz, L., Thornton, W.N., Weese, J. and Zaidan, O.F., 2009. "Joshua: An open source toolkit for parsing-based machine translation." In Proceedings of the Fourth Workshop on Statistical Machine Translation (pp. 135-139). Association for Computational Linguistics.

Linard, A., Daille, B. and Morin, E., 2015. Attempting to bypass alignment from comparable corpora via pivot language. In Proceedings of the Eighth Workshop on Building and Using Comparable Corpora (pp. 32-37).

Liu, C., Dahlmeier, D. and Ng, H.T., 2010, July. TESLA: Translation evaluation of sentences with linear-programming-based analysis. In Proceedings of the Joint Fifth Workshop on Statistical Machine Translation and MetricsMATR (pp. 354-359). Association for Computational Linguistics.

Liu, C.H., Silva, C.C., Wang, L. and Way, A., 2018, October. Pivot Machine Translation Using Chinese as Pivot Language. In China Workshop on Machine Translation (pp. 74-85). Springer, Singapore.

Mace, J., Roelke, R. and Fonseca, R., 2018. Pivot tracing: Dynamic causal monitoring for distributed systems. ACM Transactions on Computer Systems (TOCS), 35(4), p.11.

Manning, Christopher D., Mihai Surdeanu, John Bauer, Jenny Finkel, Steven J. Bethard, and David McClosky. 2014. "The Stanford CoreNLP Natural Language Processing Toolkit." In Proceedings of the 52nd Annual Meeting of the Association for Computational Linguistics: System Demonstrations, pp. 55-60.

Max, A., 2009, August. Sub-sentential paraphrasing by contextual pivot translation. In Proceedings of the 2009 Workshop on Applied Textual Inference (pp. 18-26). Association for Computational Linguistics.

McCoy, R.T. and Frank, R., 2018. Phonologically Informed Edit Distance Algorithms for Word Alignment with Low-Resource Languages. Proceedings of the Society for Computation in Linguistics (SCiL) 2018, pp.102-112.

Miura, A., Neubig, G., Sakti, S., Toda, T. and Nakamura, S., 2015. Improving pivot translation by remembering the pivot. In Proceedings of the 53rd Annual Meeting of the Association for Computational Linguistics and the 7th International Joint Conference on Natural Language Processing (Volume 2: Short Papers) (Vol. 2, pp. 573-577).

More, R., Kunchukuttan, A., Bhattacharyya, P. and Dabre, R., 2015. Augmenting Pivot based SMT with word segmentation. In Proceedings of the 12th International Conference on Natural Language Processing (pp. 303-307).

Moulinier, I., 2004. Thomson Legal and Regulatory at NTCIR-4: Monolingual and Pivot-Language Retrieval Experiments. In NTCIR.

Muraki, K., NEC Corp, 1987. Pivot-type machine translating system comprising a pragmatic table for checking semantic structures, a pivot representation, and a result of translation. U.S. Patent 4,635,199.

Nakayama, H. and Nishida, N., 2017. Zero-resource machine translation by multimodal encoder–decoder network with multimedia pivot. Machine Translation, 31(1-2), pp.49-64.

Nakov, P. and Ng, H.T., 2009, August. Improved statistical machine translation for resource-poor languages using related resource-rich languages. In Proceedings of the 2009 Conference on Empirical Methods in Natural Language Processing: Volume 3-Volume 3 (pp. 1358-1367). Association for Computational Linguistics.

Nakov, P. and Ng, H.T., 2012. Improving statistical machine translation for a resource-poor language using related resource-rich languages. Journal of Artificial Intelligence Research, 44, pp.179-222.

Nakov, P. and Tiedemann, J., 2012, July. Combining word-level and character-level models for machine translation between closely-related languages. In Proceedings of the 50th Annual Meeting of the Association for Computational Linguistics: Short Papers-Volume 2 (pp. 301-305). Association for Computational Linguistics.

Nasution, A.H., Murakami, Y. and Ishida, T., 2019. Generating Similarity Cluster of Indonesian Languages with Semi-Supervised Clustering. International Journal of Electrical and Computer Engineering (IJECE), 9(1), pp.1-8.

Nasution, A.H., Syafitri, N., Setiawan, P.R. and Suryani, D., 2017, September. Pivot-based hybrid machine translation to support multilingual communication. In Culture and Computing (Culture and Computing), 2017 International Conference on (pp. 147-148). IEEE.

Nasution, A. H., Murakami, Y., & Ishida, T. (2018). Designing a collaborative process to create bilingual dictionaries of Indonesian ethnic languages. In Proceedings of the Eleventh International Conference on Language Resources and Evaluation (LREC-2018).

Ng, E.L., Yeo, A.W. and Ranaivo-Malançon, B., 2009, December. Identification of closely related indigenous languages: An orthographic approach. In Asian Language Processing, 2009. IALP'09. International Conference on (pp. 230-235). IEEE.

Nguyen, H.T., Boitet, C. and Sérasset, G., 2007. PIVAX, an online contributive lexical data base for heterogeneous MT systems using a lexical pivot. SNLP, Bangkok, Thailand.

Norén, N. and Linell, P., 2013. Pivot constructions as everyday conversational phenomena within a cross-linguistic perspective: An introduction. Journal of Pragmatics, 54, pp.1-15.

Okumura, A., Muraki, K. and Akamine, S., 1991. Multi-lingual sentence generation from the PIVOT interlingua. In MT summit III.

Otero, P.G. and Campos, J.R.P., 2010, March. Automatic generation of bilingual dictionaries using intermediary languages and comparable corpora. In International Conference on Intelligent Text Processing and Computational Linguistics (pp. 473-483). Springer, Berlin, Heidelberg.

Papineni K., Roukos S., Ward T., & Zhu W.-J. 2001. Bleu: a method for automatic evaluation of machine translation, RC22176 Technical Report, IBM T.J. Watson Research Center.

Paul, M. and Sumita, E., 2011. Translation quality indicators for pivot-based statistical mt. In Proceedings of 5th International Joint Conference on

Natural Language Processing (pp. 811-818).

Paul, M., Finch, A. and Sumita, E., 2013. How to choose the best pivot language for automatic translation of low-resource languages. ACM Transactions on Asian Language Information Processing (TALIP), 12(4), p.14.

Paul, M., Finch, A., Dixon, P.R. and Sumita, E., 2011, July. Dialect translation: integrating Bayesian co-segmentation models with pivot-based SMT. In Proceedings of the First Workshop on Algorithms and Resources for Modelling of Dialects and Language Varieties (pp. 1-9). Association for Computational Linguistics.

Paul, M., Yamamoto, H., Sumita, E. and Nakamura, S., 2009, May. On the importance of pivot language selection for statistical machine translation. In Proceedings of Human Language Technologies: The 2009 Annual Conference of the North American Chapter of the Association for Computational Linguistics, Companion Volume: Short Papers (pp. 221-224). Association for Computational Linguistics.

Paul, S., Tandon, M., Joshi, N. & Mathur, I. 2013. "Design of a rule based Hindi lemmatizer." Proceedings of Third International Workshop on Artificial Intelligence, Soft Computing and Applications, Chennai, India.

Pierce, J. R., & Carroll, J. B. 1966. Language and machines: Computers in translation and linguistics.

Prabhumoye, S., Tsvetkov, Y., Black, A.W. and Salakhutdinov, R., 2018. Style Transfer Through Multilingual and Feedback-Based Back-Translation. arXiv preprint arXiv:1809.06284.

Ramírez, J., Asahara, M. and Matsumoto, Y., 2013. Japanese-Spanish thesaurus construction using English as a pivot. arXiv preprint arXiv:1303.1232.

Salehi, B. and Cook, P., 2013. Predicting the compositionality of multiword expressions using translations in multiple languages. In Second Joint Conference on Lexical and Computational Semantics (* SEM), Volume 1: Proceedings of the Main Conference and the Shared Task: Semantic Textual Similarity (Vol. 1, pp. 266-275).

Saralegi, X., Manterola, I. and San Vicente, I., 2012. Building a Basque-Chinese Dictionary by Using English as Pivot. In LREC (pp. 1443-1447).

Saralegi, X., Manterola, I. and Vicente, I.S., 2011, July. Analyzing methods for improving precision of pivot based bilingual dictionaries. In Proceedings of the Conference on Empirical Methods in Natural Language Processing (pp. 846-856). Association for Computational Linguistics.

Scheutz, H., 2005. Pivot constructions in spoken German. Syntax and lexis in conversation. Studies in the use of linguistic resources in talkininteraction. John Benjamins: Amsterdam, pp.103-128.

Seo, H.W., Kwon, H.S., Cheon, M.A. and Kim, J.H., 2014. Bilingual Multi-Word Lexicon Construction via a Pivot Language. Journal of Contemporary Engineering Sciences, 7(23), pp.1225-1233.

Singhoff, F., Plantec, A., Rubini, S., Gaudel, V., Li, S., Fotsing, C., Lemarchand, L., Dissaux, P. and Legrand, J., 2019. How architecture description languages help schedulability analysis: a return of experience from the Cheddar project.

Steinberger, J., Lenkova, P., Ebrahim, M., Ehrmann, M., Hurriyetoglu, A., Kabadjov, M., Steinberger, R., Tanev, H., Zavarella, V. and Vázquez, S., 2011, June. Creating sentiment dictionaries via triangulation. In Proceedings of the 2nd workshop on computational approaches to subjectivity and sentiment analysis (pp. 28-36). Association for Computational Linguistics.

Stroustrup, B., 2005. A rationale for semantically enhanced library languages. Proceedings of Library-Centric Software Design (LCSD'05).

Stuckenschmidt, J.E.H., 2003. The'family of languages' approach to semantic interoperability. Knowledge transformation for the semantic web, 95, p.49.

Tanaka, R., Murakami, Y. and Ishida, T., 2009, July. Context-Based Approach for Pivot Translation Services. In IJCAI (Vol. 2009, pp. 1555-1561).

Tiedemann, J., 2012, April. Character-based pivot translation for under-resourced languages and domains. In Proceedings of the 13th Conference of the European Chapter of the Association for Computational Linguistics (pp. 141-151). Association for Computational Linguistics.

Tsunakawa, T., Okazaki, N. and Jun'ichi Tsujii, 2008b. Building Bilingual Lexicons using Lexical Translation Probabilities via Pivot Languages. In LREC.

Tsunakawa, T., Okazaki, N. and Tsujii, J.I., 2008a. Building a bilingual lexicon using phrase-based statistical machine translation via a pivot language. Coling 2008: Companion volume: Posters, pp.127-130.

Tsunakawa, T., Okazaki, N., Liu, X. and Tsujii, J.I., 2009. A Chinese-Japanese lexical machine translation through a pivot language. ACM Transactions on Asian Language Information Processing (TALIP), 8(2), p.9.

Utiyama, M. and Isahara, H., 2007. A comparison of pivot methods for phrase-based statistical machine translation. In Human Language Technologies 2007: The Conference of the North American Chapter of the Association for Computational Linguistics; Proceedings of the Main Conference (pp. 484-491).

Vallecillo, A., 2010, June. On the combination of domain specific modeling languages. In European Conference on Modelling Foundations and Applications (pp. 305-320). Springer, Berlin, Heidelberg.

Wang, H., Wu, H. and Liu, Z., 2006, July. Word alignment for languages with scarce resources using bilingual corpora of other language pairs. In Proceedings of the COLING/ACL on Main conference poster sessions (pp. 874-881). Association for Computational Linguistics.

Wu, H. and Wang, H., 2007. Pivot language approach for phrase-based statistical machine translation. Machine Translation, 21(3), pp.165-181.

Wushouer, M., Ishida, T. and Lin, D., 2013, September. A heuristic framework for pivot-based bilingual dictionary induction. In 2013 International Conference on Culture and Computing (Culture Computing) (pp. 111-116). IEEE.

Wushouer, M., Lin, D., Ishida, T. and Hirayama, K., 2014, December. Pivot-based bilingual dictionary extraction from multiple dictionary resources. In Pacific Rim International Conference on Artificial Intelligence (pp. 221-234). Springer, Cham.

Wushouer, M., Lin, D., Ishida, T. and Hirayama, K., 2016. A constraint approach to pivot-based bilingual dictionary induction. ACM Transactions on Asian and Low-Resource Language Information Processing, 15(1), p.4.

Wushouer, M., Lin, D., Ishida, T. and Murakami, Y., 2018. A Constraint Approach to Lexicon Induction for Low-Resource Languages. In Services Computing for Language Resources (pp. 109-123). Springer, Singapore.

Zhang, M., Duan, X., Liu, M., Xia, Y. and Li, H., 2011. Joint alignment and artificial data generation: An empirical study of pivot-based machine transliteration. In Proceedings of 5th International Joint Conference on Natural Language Processing (pp. 1207-1215).

Zhang, M., Duan, X., Pervouchine, V. and Li, H., 2010, August. Machine transliteration: Leveraging on third languages. In Proceedings of the 23rd International Conference on Computational Linguistics: Posters (pp. 1444-1452). Association for Computational Linguistics.

Zhang, W., Ming, Z., Zhang, Y., Liu, T. and Chua, T.S., 2015, January. Exploring Key Concept Paraphrasing Based on Pivot Language Translation for Question Retrieval. In AAAI (pp. 410-416).

Zhang, W.N., Ming, Z.Y., Zhang, Y., Liu, T. and Chua, T.S., 2016. Capturing the semantics of key phrases using multiple languages for question retrieval. IEEE Transactions on Knowledge and Data Engineering, 28(4), pp.888-900.

Zhu, X., He, Z., Wu, H., Wang, H., Zhu, C. and Zhao, T., 2013. Improving pivot-based statistical machine translation using random walk. In Proceedings of the 2013 Conference on Empirical Methods in Natural Language Processing (pp. 524-534).

Zhu, X., He, Z., Wu, H., Zhu, C., Wang, H. and Zhao, T., 2014. Improving pivot-based statistical machine translation by pivoting the co-occurrence count of phrase pairs. In Proceedings of the 2014 Conference on Empirical Methods in Natural Language Processing (EMNLP) (pp. 1665-1675).

Ziemski, Michal, Marcin Junczys-Dowmunt, and Bruno Pouliquen. 2016. "The United Nations Parallel Corpus v1. 0." LREC.